BLOODAXE CONTE...

France has been a dominant force in the development of European culture over the past hundred years. It has made essential contributions and advances not just in literature but in all the arts, from the novel to film and philosophy; in drama (Theatre of the Absurd), art (Cubism and Surrealism) and literary theory (Structuralism and Poststructuralism). These very different art forms and intellectual modes find a dynamic meeting-point in post-war French poetry.

Some French poets are absorbed by the latest developments in philosophy or psychoanalysis. Others explore relations between poetry and painting, between the written word and the visual image. There are some whose poetry is rooted in Catholicism, and others who have remained faithful to Surrealism, and whose poetry is bound to a life of action or political commitment.

Because it shows contemporary French poetry in a broader context, this series will appeal both to poetry readers and to anyone with an interest in French culture and intellectual life. The books themselves also provide an imaginative and exciting approach to French poets which makes them ideal study texts for schools, colleges and universities.

The series has been planned in such a way that the individual volumes will build up into a stimulating and informative introduction to contemporary French poetry, giving readers both an intimate experience of how French poets think and write, and an informed overview of what makes poetry important in France.

BLOODAXE CONTEMPORARY FRENCH POETS

Series Editors: Timothy Mathews & Michael Worton

David **Kelley** was Senior Lecturer in French and Director of Studies in Modern Languages at Trinity College, Cambridge. He died in 1999. He wrote and edited books on Baudelaire, French literary theory and modern European poetry, and published a wide range of articles on drama and French literature. He translated Théophile Gautier into English and David Gascoyne into French; co-edited and translated *The New French Poetry* (Bloodaxe Books, 1996) with Jean Khalfa; and translated Jean Tardieu's *The River Underground: Selected Poems & Prose* (Bloodaxe Books, 1991).

Timothy Mathews is Professor of French at University College London. His books include *Reading Apollinaire: Theories of Poetic Language* (Manchester University Press, 1987 & 1990) and *Literature, Art and the Pursuit of Decay in 20th Century France* (CUP, 2000), which one critic described as 'passionate essays on dissidence and generosity'. He has published many articles in English and French on the interactions of word and image in texts (poetry, prose, thought) and pictures (Cubism, Surrealism and after) of the 20th century. He is currently writing a book called *Where is Alberto Giacometti?* The first volume in this series, *On the Motion and Immobility of Douve* by Yves Bonnefoy, has an introduction by him.

Michael Worton is Vice-Provost and Fielden Professor of French Language and Literature at University College London. He has published extensively on contemporary French writers, co-edited *Intertextuality: Theories and Practices* and *Textuality and Sexuality: Reading Theories and Practices* (Manchester University Press, 1990 & 1993), published two books on Michel Tournier, and co-edited *Women's Writing in Contemporary France: New Writers, New Literatures in the 1990s*; his next book is on gender, sexuality and health-care. The second volume in the Bloodaxe Contemporary French Poets series, *The Dawn Breakers* by René Char, is introduced and translated by him.

For further details of the Bloodaxe Contemporary French Poets series, please see pages 9 and 149-156 of this book.

BLOODAXE CONTEMPORARY FRENCH POETS: 8

GÉRARD MACÉ

Wood Asleep

Bois dormant

Translated by
DAVID KELLEY
with TIMOTHY MATHEWS

Introduction by
JEAN-PIERRE RICHARD

BLOODAXE BOOKS

BLOODAXE CONTEMPORARY FRENCH POETS: 8
Gérard Macé: *Wood Asleep*

Original French texts © Gérard Macé & Éditions Gallimard
1974, 1977, 1983, 2003.
English translation © Estate of David Kelley 2003
and © Timothy Mathews 2003.
Introduction © Jean-Pierre Richard 1987, 1990, 2003.

ISBN: 1 85224 432 1

First published 2003 by
Bloodaxe Books Ltd,
Highgreen,
Tarset,
Northumberland NE48 1RP.

www.bloodaxebooks.com
For further information about Bloodaxe titles
please visit our website or write to
the above address for a catalogue.

Bloodaxe Books Ltd acknowledges
the financial assistance of
Arts Council England, North East.

Cover printing by J. Thomson Colour Printers Ltd, Glasgow.

Printed in Great Britain by
Cromwell Press Ltd, Trowbridge, Wiltshire.

CONTENTS

GENERAL EDITORS' PREFACE

The Bloodaxe Contemporary French Poets series aims to bring a broad range of post-war French poetry to as wide an English-speaking readership as possible. Most volumes in the series have been devoted to a complete, unabridged work by a poet, in order to maintain the coherence of what a poet is trying to achieve in publishing a book of poems. The translators, often poets in their own right, adopt a range of different approaches, and in every case they seek out an English that gives voice to the uniqueness of the French poems. The quality of the translations has been widely recognised: two of the titles are Poetry Book Society Recommended Translations, an award given to only four books a year translated from any language.

Each translation in the series is not just faithful to the original, but aims to recreate the poet's voice or its nearest equivalent in another language: each is a translation from French poetry into English poetry. Each book's introduction seeks to make its own statement about how and why we read poetry and think poetry. The work of each poet dovetails with others in the series to produce a living illustration of the importance of poetry in contemporary French culture.

The editors are delighted to present *Wood Asleep*. These prose poems bring together three of Gérard Macé books, and this creates a coherent, unique whole with its own character and rhythms, its own echoes, and its own engagement with the leitmotifs of Macé's thought and experience. Macé has written new pieces for inclusion in this volume to emphasise its coherence and uniqueness. Like the other titles in this series, this book appears with parallel French and English text; we hope this gives an intimate sense of the poet working with word and sensation.

TIMOTHY MATHEWS
MICHAEL WORTON
University College London

9

INTRODUCTION
Cloaks and Tombs

Reading one of Gérard Macé's recent books, *The Fortuny Cloak*, in which he weaves a winding, gossamer thread back and forth across Proust's *In Search of Lost Time*, I feel I recognise the power of a figure that had already governed the invention, images and words of some of his earlier collections. I mean the figure of the *cloak*, the initial tracing of a design at once spatial and textual, a garment whose function is to wrap itself amorously round the body of a woman, Albertine, or Oriane de Guermantes; or perhaps, Macé suggests, to replace such a body, like a fetish. This garment, designed by Fortuny from the models he found in classic Italian painters, Carpaccio, Mantegna, Titian, to be draped over the shoulders of the Venetian women of his time, then over those of Proust's heroines, is simultaneously a very personal object – framing that singular quality in the desirable – and a kind of quotation coming from a far-off, exterior realm, from a fashion which itself is inspired by a world of paintings, in any case from an art different from the one through which it is evoked in Proust. This is a first illustration of the paradox maintained and performed by Macé's work as a whole, which suggests that there is nothing more original than what is borrowed, nothing more essential than what comes to us from elsewhere. Add to this the fact that the cloak's power is derived from another two of its characteristics which each have an almost structural value: the literal force of its author's name which gives it a rich expanse of meanings (*For*tuny – gold [in French, 'l'*or*'], fate ['le *sort*'], fortune, day set like a jewel in night ['le jour sorti de nuit']); and its ability to foster a secret relation to a deep and censored level of sexual orientation. In the painting by Carpaccio from which Fortuny takes it, the garment covered the shoulders of a young man and this turns it into an unambiguous sexual sign: 'the Fortuny cloak is the ghost of Albertine, but this ghost is that of a man, young and elegant, who takes his place with so many others in the long line of feminised men.'

Let me turn to the book that precedes *The Fortuny Cloak*; I won't follow the orthodox chronology but proceed in a way that Macé indicates himself in talking about the way 'a rhyme in prose summons other words, forming a story which begins perhaps with its ending...' In *The Three Caskets* the first object, the one which triggered the dream, or the memory of a dream, or 'the memory of having dreamed', was another kind of envelope, not a cloak, but a tomb, a triple tomb in which lay a Roman girl, her doll, and her clothes. A corpse kept under glass, both protected and inaccessible: a design traced this time in a geographical landscape, that of Rome, but also taken from a complex cultural intertext – Champollion visiting Rome, Freud, Shakespeare (quoted by Freud), Kleist, Bellmer, Hitchcock, and many more...So this body is quoted just as much as imagined. And its name opens up new and dynamic perspectives: for the sepulchral doll, shut behind the glass of her sarcophagus, is destined to become, among its other metamorphoses, a mannequin displayed in a shop window or a deserted house, a woman dreaming of herself naked as a mannequin on show, and a mannequin or linguistic model in Saussure's sense too – a hidden verbal body, a skeleton of letters able to generate the craziest expansions of meaning... *Crepereia Tryphaena*: a mannequin in all senses, a mannequin of mannequins, a name which will summon up tens of other names, even more than Fortuny's name does (starting out from almost the same letters: T, R, Y, F, N...). And what, you may ask, is the Roman girl's secret? Not as easy to decipher as that of the bisexual cloak, since it relates to the obscurity of a personal story, that of the narrator of *The Three Caskets*, not of Proust's novel: a secret that probably lies, to cut a long story short (too short: I'll come back to this), in the area of loss and castration.

Going further back in Gérard Macé's work, we find *Wood Asleep*, *The Balconies of Babel*, *The Garden of Languages*, in which this leitmotif is already at work, though in a more diffuse and disguised way. In *Wood Asleep*, for example, where Macé rewrites some of Perrault's *Tales*, it is the wood, the magic density of trees and plants which forms the cloak destined to cover and protect the sleeping beauty. 'A castle of ferns and sleep in a nest of flames', an ardent breeze from Rimbaud breathes vitality into the forest which 'has closed in on a sleeping beauty with an ebony face, a dead woman with crimson make-up', 'a virgin unknowingly pregnant, mother of daylight and the dawn which soon will awaken her'. Nearby we discover the clothing of *The Ass's Skin*, the dresses of Cinderella and, in Bluebeard's castle or elsewhere, many a cupboard or casket not to be opened. *Wood Asleep* – *B*ois *d*o*r*ma*n*t in French: a wood of gold ('*or*'), maybe at bay ('aux ab*ois*'), its letters leaving their mark as they drift through the space of the collection. As for the secret or fantasy to be deciphered, perhaps they have less to do than might at first appear with any transgression (a finger pricked by a spindle, a kiss which brings rebirth) than with a pleasurable dream of seduction: the sleeping beauty acts as a screen for a sleeping man, it is the hero-narrator who is awakened to love, after a long sleep of the senses, by the kiss of the good fairy transformed into a lover: 'And so the loving woman merges with the fairy who, hiding behind the tapestry, arranges things so that she is the last to speak and her propitious words, though unable to undo the bad spell, make it less final.'

In the two collections before, the cloak of plants and trees in *Wood Asleep* had taken the equally enveloping shape of a garden, with flower-beds, 'the meadows of sleep in which the author has started dreamingly to translate', and of a theatre at the heart of this garden; there, names could be seen blossoming, etymologies, true or false, sprouting, and metaphors exploding: the Garden of Plants in Paris turning, under Macé's gaze, into a Garden of Tongues, a secret space which this time goes directly from a birth to a letter, and allows us to read, in the hollow of one and the same bed ('lit'), the link between one logothetic 'donor' and another, the slide (*lit*erature – '*litt*érature'...) from Linnaeus to Littré.

So there seems to be a certain original figure of envelopment, of containment, moving from one work to another, 'rhyming' more or less obscurely with itself. Its potential significance, its provocativeness, might lead to two apparently contradictory strategies which in fact are complicitous and often associated with one other. The first consists in respecting the integrity of the container frame to such an extent as to insert or graft into it the most valuable elements furnished by memory and dream – even, or especially, if these elements appear really tiny, as in those fairy-tales where the task is to 'get the cloak of memory to pass through the eye of a needle'. The eye of a needle: the etymology of the French word for this, '*chas*', shows us at once a mouth snapping shut, and the masculine form of 'chase' or hunting – the eye of the needle encloses or encircles, a minuscule container again, but with a hole in it allowing the thread to be swallowed by it or passed through it. And this thread, a promise of continuity, proliferates into a network through Macé's text: the thread of a discourse, or of a sequence of threaded metaphors, the threads or strands of Ophelia's hair as she is borne away by the flowing stream, the thread knotted several times round itself in passementerie, another key word in which we encounter lies ('le m*en*songe'), silence, roulette ('red, odd and *pass*...'), and the password or token passed from hand to hand.

And yet, set against this indulgence in weaving (which can also be destructive, since by pulling on the threads of words and things other words might be threaded on which contradict them, or hostile elements might thread their way through the crowd of associations); set against this indulgence, and following a classic hypothesis of Melanie Klein, language can sometimes attack the space of the original body of words much more aggressively, openly tearing it apart, dismembering it. This seems to happen with special strength in *The Garden of Languages* where the writing proceeds by little discontinuous spurts, a sequence of short parentheses which are never closed, diversions – which turn out to be dead-ends – in the form and meaning of words: Macé has placed under the sign of Babel (in which he finds the very stamp of our modernity) this heterogeneous multiplicity of impious little discourses. He makes no bones about the polemical intention behind this: 'from the balcony of Babel, we watch the scramble for the cardinal mother', 'a slow explosion of words under the veil ready to open but less original than the old woman who lived in a shoe and her horizon of baggy pants'. Faced with this explosive impulse there is no cardinal mother possible, but the invasion of a crowd of voices from elsewhere, words arriving from other texts, from multiple 'donors' – Mallarmé, Rimbaud, Nerval, Roussel, Ponge, Dante, Freud, Perrault, Paulhan… – who occupy, through hidden or disguised borrowings, through quotation, allusion, pastiche, parody and imitation, both overall and in detail, the space that has now been evacuated of a personal way of writing. There is no writing subject, thinks Macé, outside of a certain kind of otherness: a movement which at one and the same time displaces, misappropriates, and disappropriates the place in which a person writes. The writer is a 'mottler of languages' ('mottling: term used in weaving. To mottle: to give different colours to the warp threads, and arrange them so that the finished piece shows a pattern', according to Littré). He weaves, then, but he weaves difference. Or, to take another metaphor, he sees himself as the locus of a word that is 'prompted', at once dream-like and erudite; his vocation is as it were an e-vocation. Hence Macé's liking for theatre, where everything is role-playing and mask, where nobody can claim possession of his or her discourse or even face, where the principal figure is the prompter, as obsessive a character as he is empty. A 'ventriloquist' poet, an 'ape', or even a parrot, sometimes discouraged by this abdication of all initiative: 'he doesn't know why he took it into his head to look like a parrot among all the dead voices'. Perhaps close encounters with dead voices restore him to his own proper (or improper) truth, which is, within himself, the death and always deferred return of a writer. The most familiar culture thus always preserves its strangeness for Macé, and that is why it never reveals its sources, is always wrapped in mystery; it is there less to be recognised than to be misrecognised, it uproots you, but so as to enable you to put down roots in the 'other' country where writing takes place.

This is certainly a powerful and persistent movement but not one, or so it seems to me, that exhausts all aspects of the work: for, however piecemeal or prompted you might have it, the cardinal body, cloak or tomb, continues nonetheless to exist. Especially in more recent works, the effort it requires, its propagation of letters and its invention of metaphors, ends up reinforcing it rather than dissolving it. It is as though the labour of the text, and of the intertext that branches out from it, were always intent on returning to this body or cloak, after many a more or less distant and adventure-filled excursion. Something Macé once wrote about Champollion and the way he learned to read summarises this tendency quite well: 'Champollion learned to read by himself using the letters in the catchwords [in French, catchword is 'réclame'] of old books. These words, often reduced to their last syllable, detached at the foot of the page and repeated at the head of the following one, helped the reader not to keep the thread and allowed Champollion to find, by trial and error, the voices of the alphabet...' The catchword is thus a *literal* return: using it as a starting-point, a whole language can be reconstituted (French at first for Champollion, then Egyptian). But it is also, Littré tells us, beyond this further adventure of the thread, another incarnation of the voice, and even the hunt (that art of displacement, of the pursuit of the *other*): the word 'réclame' can mean catchword, but also cue – 'for the prompter it is the last words of a declamatory speech, and for the hunter it is the cry recalling the hawk to the lure or the wrist'.

Now Macé's text often obeys this law of the catchword or cue: a local variation, a return to an initial object, theme or word. What is the verbal instrument of this exercise, the technique which sends the hawk flying off and then brings it back? Not metaphor, which Macé quite justly declares to be 'stateless', since it alienates its base and rips it up from the ground. Rather, homology, a figure of balance, capable of unleashing and then always bringing back to source the flow of similarities. This is how *The Fortuny Cloak* is developed, with a great deal of invention and subtlety: here Macé discovers a multiple analogon of *In Search of Lost Time*, an object (almost) capable of reflecting all that work's aspects. For example, an analogy can be posited between the – ambiguous – weave of the garment and the real substance of the novel, the essence of Proustian temporality: 'The clothes of the Venetian artist are the adornments of time lost and rediscovered on the inside – a time whose apparent thickness and unreal lightness they share.' At once a part (an embellishment or 'adornment') of the work, and the image of one of its principal aspects. But also the image of the labour carried out by the novel, of its power of aesthetic assimilation, of its existential freedom of combination: 'What Proust rediscovered in the Venetian painter was a method of constructing the work similar to his own: transposed borrowings, distant imitations (...), but above all that overall view which enables giddying juxtapositions in space and time to be made'. And such juxtapositions never cease to be forged between the cloak and the work: both are subject to the same balance of tradition and invention, for 'the book itself is also an adornment whose front and back covers are related as the dead to the living, the old to the new', to the point where Macé sees the author Proust as wrapped up in his work, or in the memory which is spinning that work, a bit like Albertine was in the fabric of her cloak (or, in Venice, as the narrator imagines, in her shroud): 'As for the author who is exhibiting himself, he is never entirely naked, but wrapped in the folds of his memory, or disguised as a donor, thanks to an art which is always an art of borrowing.' It would be easy to quote many similar passages, in which homology playfully operates on every level, radiating out in every direction of the work. The cloak is used there as a sort of material and cultural 'etymon' or origin, able to organise the most diverse aspects of Proust's novel around itself, by an almost boundless set of variations on similarity. Its singular texture makes it a perfect mirror of the text.

And of what is outside the text, too: for the homological power of evocation held by such an object does not end with the work in which we meet it. Across the name *Fortuny*, taken alliteratively as a window ('fenêtre'), a literal frame or, once more, the eye of a needle, we see the *Orient* showing off its gold ('*or*') and its double perspective, Jewish and Persian: it is a world which, moreover, returns most vividly in *In Search of Lost Time* with the characters of Esther (in her Racinian incarnation, played by girls disguised as men...) and Sheherazade (the eternal storyteller, just as Marcel's mother is the original reader of stories, the one who really gives her *voice* to Proust's narrative). But it is above all in *The Three Caskets* where we see the practice of external, intertextual or even intercultural homology in full bloom. For the march towards the three little unearthed sarcophagi and the secrets that can be read in them is meant to be an exact parallel to Freud's advance on Rome (it is well known how difficult this was), and to the reading of Freud's text 'The Theme of the Three Caskets' (via Shakespeare), with the whole aspect of pilgrimage and impossible possession that such experiences involved: 'Coming from Orvieto, where the veined marble, the green of the lizards, the sense of loss and the summer all combine to create the impression that forgetting a word, a fragment of poetry or of a proper name is a possibility overlooking an abyss...' The gold ('*or*') of O*r*vieto (associated with an alliterative line of v's: '*v*enant, *v*einé, *v*ert' ('coming, veined, green') glitters, as in F*or*tuny (musically linked, moreover, to O*r*vieto), or Wood Asleep ('Bois D*or*mant'), thus illuminating the traveller's advance into the space of his own enigma. But it is also Freud's advance, as he interprets the forgetting of the name of Sign*or*elli (the painter, in Orvieto, of the end of the world), or of the adjective *aliquis* in a line of poetry by Virgil, after the opening word, *exoriare* (referring to the woman whose period is late, the fear of a birth, the miracle of Saint Januarius). To these summons of death and birth is associated a more animal image of desire, that of the *green lizard*, the one which escaped from between the feet of *Gradiva*. So here we have, so to speak, a condensation of allusions, further enriched by the narrative developments devoted to Hannibal and Champollion, two of Freud's great heroes too, the one because he never decided to enter Rome, the other because, like Freud and the unconscious, he was the first to discover the key to hieroglyphics.

The entire complicated game of these resemblances, intersections and cross-references is confirmed and even brought into being by the dissemination of the letters contained in the name of the dead girl, *Crepereia Tryphaena*, a dissemination which never takes the shape of a scattering, but which suggests, instead, encounters, half-surprising coincidences. For what can one actually hear in this name and this nickname? 'The alliteration,' writes Macé, 'of desire and a secret divulged in the heart of words, but also the anagram of a living name', or even, he specifies elsewhere, of the forenames of various women linked to the narrator by love or family relationship. Other texts make us think of Anne, the 'annamourous wife', of Irène, and who else? The alliteration of desire and secret could refer to *crypt, father* ('père') (*priapic*, since we are in Rome?...) The name's formula also functions, as I said earlier, as a mannequin, starting with the momentum of its first two consonants, *cr*, which refer to so many words that begin in the same way and is linked, moreover, to elements of the story being told. This formula recalls the storms that *cr*ackled over Rome that summer, the *cr*inkly hair miraculously blossoming round the skeleton's skull (in fact, plants growing in the water that submerges it: but this miracle also refers to one of the founding gestures in Macé's family mythology, that by which an 'illiterate grandmother', for lack of mirrors, would comb her hair over a bucket of water in a farmyard); it evokes the power of the *cr*epuscular or twilight hours, the tensing up ('*cr*ispation') of writing ('*écr*iture'); and the initial two letters, combined this time with the final *a*, create a frame (the eye of a needle, a cloak, a mannequin, whatever you prefer) for other possible forenames: *Clélia, Christina, Cordelia*.

This is a good example of Macé's choosiness, the extremely selective trend underlying his literal inventiveness. For of these names he abandons the first two, which would not have lead him to any of his favourite territories (unless I am mistaken there is no echo of Stendhal in his texts), so as to keep the third, which gleams with another gold ('or') and brings him back to Shakespeare: not the Shakespeare of *The Merchant of Venice* in which Freud read the story of *The Three Caskets* (with its beautiful formula, of great importance to Macé – as we shall see – evoking a humbly luminous silence: 'Thy paleness moves me more than eloquence...'), but the Shakespeare of *King Lear* in which Cordelia devotes herself to the old king, lost amid the 'tempest and the invisible storms he struggles with, his shoulders bare beneath the ermine mantle, trembling with rage and shaken by madness'. The daughter has become the mantle, the living cloak, of her father. But the latter was linked in yet another way to Macé's family legend: via the character of his grandfather Jules Galles, with his Roman emperor's name – 'a day labourer from the North, with his bundle on his shoulder' – and beside whom, as he lay 'bedridden, dying, pouring out insults and profanities', Macé first read *King Lear*.

Macé's work thus seems tempted as much by similarity as by otherness – a similarity that, moreover, easily goes astray amid the mirrors and doubles; it simultaneously seeks displacement and encounter, an encounter that would displace and then demand new encounters; it aims to combine loss of momentum and over-determination. This appears nowhere more clearly than in one of the areas in which the invention in Macé's work is most evidently grounded, that of imagining the body: the author's body, that of some persons close to him (sister, mother, father, childhood friends or neighbours), the bodies of a few cherished writers – Nerval, Mallarmé, Rimbaud, Corbière, Segalen, all the heroes of that fine collection of critical essays, *Ex libris*. How should we talk about this body, obsessional as it is here, as often as not bowed down with anguish, and, in addition, endowed with an extreme *credibility* for the reader, a great capacity for *contagion*? Three remarks could be made about this body, three 'catchwords' once again, and the three of them together would illuminate one of the aspects of poetic originality: first the emotional support or grounding that this body provides for all those 'prompter's whispers'; then the way it has of defining itself, even amid all the repetitions, by the violence of a void, a rent which ceaselessly tears it away elsewhere, beside itself; finally the relation this wound, a painful hollow, has with the activity of poetry. For it is true, as we are shown with precision and passion – no longer via the language of a commonplace – that the poem here is written directly into the body, for want of the body, to quote a favourite phrase of Mallarmé – perhaps in the body's failure, Gérard Macé might comment in his turn. If in any case the body can dream of itself as the first cloak of our lives, it is a cloak full of holes, always disintegrating, already a virtual tomb, riddled by mortality. It is for us to recognise as much in the domain foregrounded here – that of anatomy.

Let me consider a key leitmotif – the foot, in the scene Macé often repeats, with the roles sometimes varied, where a younger sister twists her ankle: 'the dance of a sister learning to walk, whose foot twists and lands her flat on her back.' This twist leads directly to a certain way of writing: 'poetry which hobbles in prose and which is no longer supported by the *scribe's apparatus*', the discourse betrayed by the 'the invisible "padding" of a lame and rickety sentence.' And these homonymic derivations have soon summoned new heroines to their aid: 'Around the bruised foot of the dancing girl (what twelve- or thirteen-year-old Gradiva doomed to infanticide, or some Cinderella trying on a man's shoe?), the bandages that one undoes merge with the festoons of the sentence.' The fantasy of castration of the lower extremities – one 'foot' less – also summons the most charming and fleet-footed or dancing actresses and submits them to the same broken destiny. But the bandages, also originating in the Egyptian dream (images of a mummy unwrapped and resuscitated), promise both a cure and a literary solution, since their shape can, with a little indulgence (as psychoanalysts talk of somatic indulgence) evoke the wandering gait of a discourse.

This fracture is even more serious, but also rich with possibilities, when it attacks the very place in which words are framed: the throat, the lips. Several episodes from childhood seem here to have the force of a traumatic memory: probably an operation on the tonsils, when 'as in a dream the bleeding organs of speech had to be opened, an incision which precedes a series of memories in red ink: a rabbit being skinned, a hen being bled with a pair of scissors, and my mother on her haunches in the farmyard.' The mother organises this entire drama of blood before undergoing it herself in a dream of deflowering which we will encounter in a moment. A juxtaposed episode arranges the same nightmare slightly differently, but repeats with just as much force: the one in which the voice is not affected from the outside, but breaks as it were from inside itself, as the result of some tension, some excess into which it has thrown itself. The obsessional disaster of the song resembles an haemorrhage. 'His mother was a singer, and this woman's disturbing song, when she reached the highest notes, caused such heavy bleeding in her throat that it was weeks before she could sing again. So, the minute she started to sing, everyone would run home to hide, so as not to hear any of those heart-rending notes, not to have to undergo the sharpness of that wound.' Is there any escape in writing from such a catastrophe? Of course, and an exemplary escape at that, since perhaps the greatest writers have experienced it: aphasia, muteness (or its attenuated version, the stammer): Mallarmé strangled by a spasm in the larynx, Baude-laire and his 'Goddammit Goddammit' ('Crénom, Crénom'...), Nerval hanging from his street lamp, for 'the strangled voice is perhaps also a dream of being hanged'.

Why should such a theoretical importance be granted – over and above its status as fantasy – to strangulation and muteness? The reason is that, as another original scene – that of adolescence – tells us, the boy becomes mute when his voice breaks ('mue'); he becomes other, learning the name of his father (who was himself a bastard, an illegitimate child) next to the fountain (or the wash-house) where he has hitherto gazed at his reflection. So the poet is the one who falls silent, at the risk of dying as a result: like the heroine of a novella by Balzac, a woman who becomes amnesiac and aphasic after crossing the Beresina, he can drag just one last cry from himself, a 'barely articulated cry', 'a word drunk on vowels', the word *Adieu*, 'which all by itself summarises an entire story.' For, in contrast to the stifling effect of consonants, an ill-starred leitmotif in Macé, vowels have an emancipatory power: they come closest to articulating the sounds of wind and silence, and so provide the best escape from the old chatter, and, in the very ditty of death, the best hope of reaching another diction, perhaps another life.

These are a few extreme aspects of a syndrome which can also take more benign forms: nearest to the throat, for example, that deformation of the mouth, that cut of the lips which seems to affect the paternal figures and other derivative characters, Crepereia's doll for example. This leads to an accent, an inability to speak – or to love – properly: it is the 'old infirmity of the lips in the skewed pronunciations and kisses without hope', the lisp which perhaps stops you pronouncing the password correctly, saying – in the Bible – *S*ibboleth instead of *S*hibboleth (or the opposite). But even there, castration, while excluding and condemning, opens up elsewhere onto other existential resources; not being able to speak properly is perhaps just a discreet mode of silence: it is in any case inextricably linked to everything that lives on ambiguity, error, clumsiness – dream, for instance, and poetry too: there is a power in 'the accent produced by a harelip and the voice which lisps between wakening and sleep, as familiar as poetry when it returns without warning, with its rhymes and reminiscences, prime and terce, the double lilac on the edge of the meadow.'

Finally we need to think of the organ which moves not the voice but writing: the hand. The hand too is short of poetry the minute it is doubled, deviated, made gauche, the hand of a thwarted left-hander, or a hand which writes its language like a foreign language, in *italics* for example. Or, even more brutally, a hand that's been amputated, deprived of a finger, like the father's (and that of the master-spy in Hitchcock's *The Thirty-Nine Steps*), or severed, becoming a 'hand of glory', as in a novella by Nerval on which Macé's work gives an exemplary commentary. For once again, cutting opens up onto a truth of the other – an otherness in which the reader will lodge, in turn, everything that is unknown in his or her own life: 'One of the author's hands does not belong to him: it is the hand *possessed* of a biographer unknown to himself. This biographer is the other in the self, the left-handed man who is making ready the place which the reader will come to occupy, so as to read – over my shoulder as it were – the lines of my hand.' Reading as palmistry. And writing as possession, but one which dispossesses, leading to the *terra incognita* of an as yet undiscovered biography.

For the poems of Macé are not content, even across the multiplicity of intertexts, with writing the body, with the writing of the body, or the body painfully exposed to writing. This only has any sense when taken up into a history, a sequence of family events dreamed or remembered, linked to 'the secret of filiation, that sort of blason which memory seeks in vain to gild anew'. This history that needs a new layer of gilt or gold (here again is the beloved 'gold' ['or'], and with the first syllable back-to-front, the family *ro*mance, which this history provides a defintition of here) is a history that Macé's texts give us to read, or at least guess at, in the form of reiterated fragments or flashes which often draw openly, and at one remove as it were, on the concepts and operations of psychoanalysis: we find for example Oedipus at his crossroads (or between the two thieves!), the prostitute mother, castration (it threatens the 'slender virile reason' of Mallarmé's Hamlet), the primal scene (the 'sighs of the saint and the fairy's cries' imported from Nerval and implanted in rustic scenes of closed bedrooms and bloody bedclothes). But these elements take shape and conviction from a really fundamental discrepancy: for the imagined hero of the family structure is not, at least does not seem to be, based on what we glimpse, the son, but his father with whom he often identifies – a father who himself is a bastard, an illegitimate son, and who received his name (and thus that of the narrator) from the man who had adopted him after marrying his mother.

From this there spring several essential scenes, whose shock reverberates across the entire space of the work. That of the wedding for instance, the mother's marriage (in reality that of the grandmother, the 'adulterous woman'), with 'the humiliation of the child faced with a couple of married parents': for the son is there too, carrying in his arms – and this throws new light on the leitmotif – a doll with which he ends up identifying: 'On the ground, I pick a wretched piece of wood wrapped in a cloth: the poor boy's doll which a child born out of wedlock had to bear round on the wedding day of his father with a woman he has no recollection of. When his voice breaks another man gives him his name. It's that name which I bear today.' A name picked up (*'ramassé'*), then, as the text points out (Gérard Macé), just as Fortuny's name was, with the help of *In Search of Lost Time*…The author's name, furthermore, turns out to be wrongly copied, misspelt, in the registry office records.

Going further back, this fantasmatic recreation reaches beyond the wedding scene to the obscure moments of nativity and conception.

Sacred history and art history enable the author to imagine an immaculate conception, since there wasn't any real father, with the intervention of a deflowering angel, a sly and rather rascally character running off across the farmyard: 'the oaths uttered by the angel (who is put there perhaps just for the lover of our mothers) when he came to wash from the tile the trace of blood which preceded the annunciation.' As for the nativity, it is dreamed in the scene at Bethlehem, reconstructed through the strange forenames of the father, the illegitimate son, which declare at one and the same time conjugal deception, a sort of inversion of birth, and identification with a mothering virginity: 'I had the presentiment of words without vowels' (Macé seems to take his name as heavily consonantal, especially when the M and the C are read in it as Roman figures), 'and of a secret too heavy to bear for a father with unpronounceable names: Léon born backwards, Joseph with ass's ears, Mary pregnant all over again.'

From this family history or prehistory, real or imaginary, what emerges or re-emerges for life and writing, the writing of life, the life of writing? An atmosphere of guilt, the sense of disorder, the vertigo of loss. Guilt? Present everywhere, even more than usually, it affects every moment and every actor in the family scene: the guilty 'mistake' of the mother, to start with, transformed into the spelling mistake of the scribe copying out the name, or that of the son learning how to write, and thereby betraying the secret, or refusing to acknowledge the birth of a little sister (he writes – another of the work's refrains – 'the last-born girl' ['la née dernière'] for 'last year' ['l'année dernière']). The disorder comes from that slip in the cogs of the machinery, that generation which has to fit into the architecture of the Oedipus complex while perversely distorting every one of its roles. The family romance, for instance, really is played out since the father-son is a bastard and loses his virtues of compensation or fictional development and falls into a reality that resists all conceptualisation. The illegitimate father-son, that 'contumacious husband' (Corbière, quoted by Macé), or that social bastard, that freedman (in the case of the husband of Crepereia, with his initial letter L, 'liber', free, as in the case of the name Léon), could be either an Oedipus or a Jesus, or even, humorously (Macé is happy to indulge), both at once. While the feminine figures tend to meld – mother, 'guilty' grandmother, other feminine forebears, aunts – in the same shameful cloak, paternity is experienced, on two or three levels, as a 'family quarrel', where nobody is sure who is attacking and who is defending, nor what the real object of the battle might be: 'Why does it always turn out when writing that reason should fail so dismally, and from the oldest legends onwards should murder the man it wanted to avenge?'

But especially 'the biographical flaw', already detected in a Segalen, for instance, a kind of rent in the great cloak-tomb of genealogical precedence, forces the author to experience the dimension of the family past as a loss. In Macé's finest pages, the desire for origin comes back to a cemetery in the Île-de-France where all that can be read on the tombstones are the humble names of forgotten friends or neighbours: 'Annezo, Santhune, Bilgris, Réguéda, Sainte-Beuve and Labrunie' (neighbours in literature too, then), almost anonymous names, and yet princely names too, able to give their support, in their lordly destitution or humility, to the future of a writing which will itself long to be plain and poor: 'But I was forgetting other kings in velvet drawers, other queens in aprons: Léontine Donnée, Jules Cézeur and Gervaise Vidor: it's among all these names that I come to glean assonances and rhymes far from rich, for they compose an *ars poetica* without commentary.'

Without commentary. And this present commentary – should I now bring it to a close, or maybe even never have begun it? I should in any case end by highlighting a simple fact: the link between the pleasure and the difficulty of writing, on the one hand, with all those elements of disorder and breakage, here and there, in the imaginary realm of the body and that of the family ('evocation' itself, and the refusal to assume one's own voice, are perhaps linked to the discrepancy, to the genealogical 'flaw' I mentioned). For from the moment the child learns to write, the 'broken sticks' of writing continue to register pain, and in every poem language makes a 'turbid water' flow, as that in La Fontaine's fox fable. Macé seems to think, with Melanie Klein and many others, that we write to repair a broken body, a torn cloak, but our writing is itself a kind of tearing. One of the characters of his mythology is the embalmer, in whose house it is – in a repeated riddle – forbidden to blaspheme, to *bestemmiare* (or perhaps, by virtue of a false etymology, to 'behave in a beastly way', as one 'behaves angelically', and we know what a dubious role the angel plays...). But more than embalming the lost body in the cloak of memory, it is perhaps a matter of placing it in the tomb, as Corbière does (in his case, it is also the bier of his own body): 'The funereal italics of the "Posthumous sonnet" mark the triumph of the other, the double, weary of tossing and turning within us. The triumph of the book too, that shroud which we weave in the cross-threads of writing. Thinking that we are sewing up a deep wound in ourselves, we are with our own hands aiding the work of death, which resembles that of a birth.' Let us not interpret this death-life religiously. Remember, instead, what Lévinas writes about Derrida, the grand master of the prompted word: 'the reversal of conceptualising limit into a precondition, of defect into source, of abyss into the possibility of existence, of discourse into a space', and 'the reversal of this reversal itself into a destiny'. In a less metaphysical and more voluptuous way, we could say that nobody is stopping us wrapping ourselves in a kind of unbinding – and we could repeat the words of *The Three Caskets*, with their undeniable charm, in which desire slips into and encloses itself in the perfectly disordered material of its associations: 'This image was disturbed by another, originating in a dream I had broken into, the dream of a woman who at my bidding had shared confidences with me, *listening in the way one wraps oneself up in the sheets of an unmade bed.*' Perhaps that is also how readers and critics should read.

JEAN-PIERRE RICHARD
translated by Andrew Brown

Selected Bibliography

The books listed here are in French. Except for *Leçon de chinois*, neither Gérard Macé nor Jean-Pierre Richard has been translated into English before.

GÉRARD MACÉ: **Books**

Le jardin des langues (Paris: Gallimard, 1974)
Les balcons de Babel (Paris: Gallimard, 1977)
Ex Libris (Paris: Gallimard, 1980)
Leçon de chinois (Montpellier: Fata Morgana, 1981)
   [translated as *Chinese Lesson* by David Kelley in *The New French Poetry*, edited by David Kelley & Jean Khalfa (Bloodaxe Books, 1996)]
Bois dormant (Paris: Gallimard, 1983)
Les trois coffrets (Paris: Gallimard, 1985)
Le manteau de Fortuny (Paris: Gallimard, 1987)
Le dernier des Égyptiens (Paris: Gallimard, 1988; Folio, 1997)
Vies antérieures (Paris: Gallimard, 1991)
La mémoire aime chasser dans le noir (Paris: Gallimard, 1993)
Choses rapportées du Japon, photographs by Pierre Alechinsky (Fontfroide: Fata Morgana, 1993)
Cinéma muet, drawings by Pierre Alechinsky (Fontfroide: Fata Morgana, 1995)
L'autre hémisphère du temps (Paris: Gallimard, 1995)
Le singe et le miroir, original drawings by Sam Szafran (Cognac: Le temps qu'il fait, 1998)
La photographie sans appareil (Cognac: Le temps qu'il fait, 2001)
Un détour par l'Orient (Paris: Le Promeneur, 2001)
Le goût de l'homme (Paris: Le Promeneur, 2002)
Bois dormant et autres poèmes en prose (Paris: Poésie/Gallimard, 2002)

Criticism on GÉRARD MACÉ

Images et signes, Lectures de Gérard Macé, edited by Serge Boucheron, Jean-Louis Lampel & Nicolas Ragonneau (Cognac: Le Temps qu'il fait, 2001)

JEAN-PIERRE RICHARD: **Books**

Littérature et sensation: Stendhal et Flaubert (Paris: Seuil, 1954)
(Collection *Points*)

Poésie et profondeur (Paris: Seuil, 1955) (Collection *Points*)

L'Univers imaginaire de Mallarmé (Paris: Seuil, 1961)

Onze études sur la poésie moderne (Paris: Seuil, 1964)

Paysage de Chateaubriand (Paris: Seuil, 1967)

Études sur le romantisme (Paris: Seuil, 1970)

Proust et le monde sensible (Paris: Seuil, 1974)

Microlectures (Paris: Seuil, 1979)

Microlectures: pages, paysages (Paris: Seuil, 1984)

État des choses: études sur huit écrivains d'aujourd'hui (Paris: Gallimard, 1990)

Terrains de lecture (Paris: Gallimard, 1996)

TRANSLATORS' NOTE

The idea of embarking on the exciting and difficult journey of translating into English these volumes of Gérard Macé's prose poetry grew from the friendship that had developed between Gérard himself and David Kelley. Sadly, David died in 1999 before he could see this work through. As co-editor of Bloodaxe Contemporary French Poets, I was anxious for this book not to disappear as well, and so with some trepidation I immersed myself in the adventure of bringing this translation to life. Inevitably, this meant that the tonality of the English has drifted over to my own ways of reading and hearing, and I have had to find my own ways of responding in English to some of the unique intricacies of Macé's prose poetry. But what we can offer here to readers and their imagination is a genuine, dynamic, unpredictable collaboration; a collaboration between translators as well as between the translators and the author. This labour has been a long time coming through; but it has been a labour of love.

I would like to thank Laura Cordy at Trinity College, Cambridge for her painstaking work not only on preparing the final typescript, but also on the numerous drafts through which this translation evolved; and Jean Khalfa for making that possible. I would also like to thank Michael Worton for his careful reading of the final draft of this translation; and Gérard Macé especially, not only for reading the translation so helpfully and encouragingly, but also for his immense patience.

Gérard Macé has added three pieces to *Bois dormant* written after its original publication in 1983: 'Tete-bêche', 'Pierrot valet de la mort' and 'La forêt qui se met à marcher'. The introductory essay, 'Cloaks and Tombs' by Jean-Pierre Richard, was first published as 'Manteaux et tombeaux' in *Critique* (November 1987), and reprinted in *État des choses* (Gallimard, Paris, 1990). It is translated here by Andrew Brown. The editors are grateful to Jean-Pierre Richard for his kind permission to publish his essay here in English.

TIMOTHY MATHEWS

Le jardin des langues

The Garden of Languages

(1974)

Pour Annemoureuse, et pour quelques amis, ce livre qui s'est écrit selon leur lecture... Écriture de la main gauche (la main italique) *quand je croyais parler seul...*

«*Dis-moi donc quelle est la production du Zèbre antique. – Il est fait du pur destin anatomique. C'est un joli cheval zébré, et qui ressent parfois sa femelle, sans qu'ils soient rapprochés l'un de l'autre. Mais en réalité cet animal est constitué de manière à ressentir ce qui se passe au loin dans les régions polaires. Il s'habitue mal aux scènes scandaleuses des Terriens. Il nous rend à tous de très grands services. Ainsi, quand il pleut, il ne jouit pas des mêmes facultés. Il s'enterre, dans la terre, et pleure souvent, car il se ressent de sa femelle qui l'appelle au loin. Ils communiquent ensemble et nous transmettent des messages importants...*»

JEANNE TRIPIER LA PLANÈTAIRE

For Annamorous and for a few friends, this book wrote itself with an ear for their reading... Left-handed writing (the italic hand)* when I thought I was talking to myself...

* this book was set entirely in italics in the original French edition

Now tell me about the generation of the ancient Zebra. – The Zebra is made from the purest anatomical destiny. It is a pretty striped horse, and which sometimes senses his mate when neither is close. But in truth the make-up of this animal allows it to sense what is going on far away and in polar regions. It does not adapt well to the scandalous scenes of Landowners. It is extremely helpful to all of us. So for example when it rains, it does not enjoy the same faculties. It buries itself, and buried in the earth it often weeps, for it is affected by its mate calling him from afar. They communicate with each other and transmit important messages to us...

JEANNE TRIPIER LA PLANÈTAIRE

I

Propriétaire d'enjambées de sept lieues et davantage je traverse vitesse
multipliée les carcans de vos têtes les régions pluvieuses de vos
conversations où les empreintes lisibles sont des coquilles émiettées
à contenance de sable (la terre n'est qu'une feuille morte longuement
mouillée de pourriture disent les uns les autres sont bâillonnés le
ciel est cet envers ordurier de la terre ou réservoir d'injures ou pelure
d'orange séchée sur un grand lit à baldaquin où roulent des coquetiers
à la renverse dont la tête en bas déverse un ancien savoir. . . . . .

*

Mémoire sera tatouée par les averses trémières d'un lieu vierge et
noir où s'enfoncent les sabots d'animaux diluviens la robe transie
par les caresses d'un clitoris (retours des banquises de la jouissance
vous n'êtes plus clandestins grâce aux oiseaux se levant l'hiver passe
dans votre traîne oiseaux de régions périmées qui vous cachaient
sous le nom de baisemains . . . .

*

Phrases mal tournées de l'horloge parlante elles sont comme l'eau du
café au passage retenant un goût de sable amer pourtant filtré de la
bouche aux reins dans lesquels circulent des rames de voyageurs tous
en leurs mains brandissant une pelle non de l'âge du fer mais de l'âge
mental celle de nos huit ans à perpétuité (la raison perdue de vivre
entre taupe et lézard court sous ma peau plus vite que le sang. . . .

*

On bat mes habits sur la pierre devant la cave la froide embouchure
où se vident les éponges (bouche fouettée par les lilas couperose
du ciel mange le cancer du sens le panier noir renversé vidant son
sable délivre le pâle inceste des mots le couple en moi de la muette
et l'effraie car je prévois le soubresaut de la bête (le fer sera battu
rouges les oiseaux la femme traversée couchera dans la mémoire
des savanes et moi roulé vif l'œil à ciel ouvert dans les chambres
sanglantes . . . .

*

I

Owner of strides seven leagues long and more I cross with multiplied speed the iron collars of your heads the rainy regions of your conversations where legible imprints are fragmented shells with the countenance of sand (the earth is but a dead leaf long soaked with rot say some the others are gagged the sky is that filthy reverse of the earth or reservoir of abuse or dried-up orange peel on a huge four-poster bed where upside-down egg-cups roll about from their upside-down heads there spills a stream of ancient knowledge. . . .

*

Memory will be tattooed by the many-bloomed showers of a black and virgin place where the hooves of diluvian animals sink into the mire a coat stiff with clitoral caresses (ice floes of pleasure returning you are clandestine no longer thanks to the birds rising winter passes in your wake birds from regions long past which hid you under the name of kiss-your-hand. . . . .

*

The speaking clock's awkward sentences turned out wrong are like coffee that keeps a flavour of bitter sand in passing in spite of being filtered from mouth to kidney where reams of passengers are all brandishing spades not from the iron age but from our everlasting mental age of eight (the meaning of life lost between mole and lizard runs under my skin faster than blood. . . . .

*

My clothes are beaten on the rock in front of the cellar the cold opening where sponges are squeezed (mouth lashed by lilacs the vitriol of the sky eats into the cancer of sense the upturned black basket emptying its sand sets free the pale incest of words the couple within me of mute woman and screech-owl for I foresee the sudden start of the beast (iron will be beaten the birds red the woman crossed will lie in the memory of the savanas and I was fleeced with my eyes open to the sky in bedrooms that were bleeding. . . . .

*

Œil natal retourné ouvre les prairies sur le livre noir et mange les caillots flambés du cœur ciel tabac refroidi chauffe à blanc les poumons au pied des murs de la mémoire et rouge le chiendent (fracture l'os et le sang s'ouvrira serruriers du soir videz-vous de la peur de la nuit vomie violette laissez-nous sur les prairies de poivre le cœur l'ogre rouge rassasié de la chair les feux éteints de l'orgie. . . . .

*

Quand l'œil aura tout vu mon corps sera creux comme l'arbre du délire où loge le hibou à faire peur je coucherai dans une horloge à la dérive à la fin fendue par une pierre pour couler sans fond dans le troisième décan de décembre (plombée par le sommeil la chute le long de l'œsophage mène aux poubelles de la mémoire en pourriture sous la langue morte elle-même prise dans la rotative affolée du sens salivant pour rien le poème papier mâché le papier des forêts permises où les ossements montraient la route (où maintenant réduits en poudre ils lavent les cerveaux pour de nouvelles morts à six pieds sous terre sous une montagne de songes ceux de l'or . . . .

*

. . . .
. . . . .les produits du sens nouveau comme vanille et cumin dans du vieux miel et la mort qui sodomise l'anus des nuits le ciel un perpétuel taureau d'étoiles (leurs couilles les pendules roses et sales dont la corne brûle entre véronique et châtiment l'anthrope l'aine offerte à déchirer le sens. . . . .

*

Déjà l'ouïe outrée du violon enfanté de la viole crève nos tympans hantés d'une chanson jadis jouée sur virginal et d'avant l'écriture la vie à vif on dirait un fruit mûr tombé de l'arbre clair de l'urine mais maintenant nu et nègre je veux arracher la langue de l'arrière-gorge et la manger crue loin des cuisines (je meurs dans une colonie toucouleur à sa vue les vigies de la parole ne pourront jamais crier «sens» elles viendront seulement ramasser l'orange pelée de ma tête en inventant la profession de croque mort. . . . .

*

Native eye upturned opens meadows onto the black book and eats the flaming clots of the heart the stale tobacco sky heats the lungs at the foot of memory to a white heat and red the couchgrass (break the bone and the blood will open locksmiths of the evening empty yourselves of the fear of the night vomited violet leave us on meadows of pepper our red ogre heart replete with flesh the extinguished fires of orgy. . . . .

*

When the eye has seen everything my body will be hollow as the tree of frenzy residence of the fearsome owl I shall sleep in a clock adrift and finally split open by a stone and sinking to fathomless depths in the last ten days of december (plumbed by sleep a fall the length of the windpipe leads to the dustbins of memory rotting under a dead tongue caught in the crazy rotary press of sense salivating to no purpose the poem pulped paper the paper of the public forests where bones showed the way (where now reduced to powder they wash brains for the new dead six feet in the ground under a mountain of dreams those of gold. . . . .

*

. . . .
. . . . .products of the new meaning like vanilla and cumin in old honey and death sodomising the nights' anus the sky a perpetual taurus of stars (their balls dirty pink pendulums whose horn burns between the matador's pass and castigation the anthropo-groin given up to tear sense apart. . . . .

*

Already the extravagance of the violin born of the viola bursts our eardrums haunted by a song once played on virginals and from before writing life flayed almost like a ripe fruit fallen from the light tree of urine but now naked and negro I want to rip the tongue from the back of my throat and eat it raw far from the kitchens (I'm dying in a tukulor colony in catching sight of it the crow's nests of speech will never cry 'sense' but only pick up the peeled orange of my head and invent the undertaker's profession. . . . . .

*

II

D'un œuf le même jour quatre mille au ventre noir de la fin mangeuse dans la nuit du miel mental Méloé me dévore jusqu'au membre gelé dans le ventre gros de la mort cachée au commencement dans les poils de ma mère sous mille métaphores de l'amour couvant des œufs noirs Méloé des alvéoles vidés de la moelle rivale de l'abeille mortelle et des insectes du sang elle est reine et veuve la femme blanche de la ruche du cœur. . . . .

*

Outre la robe l'œil retourné du mort qui mangeait dans mes régions natales maudite mémoire d'un repas chez les porcs à la lumière noire de minuit les larmes avalées par la femme vue en voyage au fond des dormeuses (calèches vers l'aube attablée pour le festin d'épluchures et sous l'œil mort de l'œdipe la femelle somnambule vos fêtes c'étaient mes tortures tournantes (ciel l'égout de guêpes le corps laissé dans l'autre et sur la bouche l'essaim de nuages suppliciés vos cris dans les caves sont le bruit des songes creux au tamis noir de l'or fin. . . . .

*

Dans les forêts permises d'un seul hémisphère le cri du coq autrement nommé cauchemar des lions c'est le lieu de parole où le cœur est reconnu coq flambé dans les champs de tabac cendre mâchée la folie la fougère crânienne consumée c'est la voûte éclairée noire d'un porche ici là c'est la bouche où se verse à crédit le prix de la peur et même le corps roué dans les chambres de joie c'est dire la proie des charniers où le cœur mange les mots sur une table de vent (je n'aurai ni cave ni tombeau mais un phalanstère d'araignées. . . . .

*

II

From a single egg in a single day hatch four thousand with the black belly of the great eater in the night of mental honey Meloe devours me to the very member frozen in the heavy belly of death hidden in the beginning in my mother's pubic hair under a thousand metaphors of love hatching black eggs Meloe of the honeycomb cells emptied of the rival marrow of the mortal bee and the blood insects she is queen and widow the white woman of the heart's hive. . . . .

*

Besides the dress the upturned eye of the dead man eating in the regions where I was born accursed memory of a meal amongst the swine in the black light of midnight the tears swallowed by the woman seen on my travels in the depths of the night carriages (barouches drawn to the dawn banquet of potato peel and under the dead eye of oedipus the sleepwalking female your feasts were the wheels of my tortures (the heavens a sewer of wasps the body left in the other and on the mouth the swarm of tortured clouds your cries in the cellars are the noise of hollow dreams passed through the black sieve of fine gold. . . . .

*

In the public forests of a single hemisphere the cry of the cock also known as the nightmare of lions is the place of words where the heart is recognised coq flambé in the tobacco fields masticated ash madness the consumed fern of the skull here is the black-lit vault of a porch there is the mouth where the price of fear is deposited on credit and even the body broken in the pleasure chambers this is prey in the charnel-houses where the heart eats the words on a table of wind (I shall have neither cellar nor tomb but a phalanstery of spiders. . . . .

*

Langue rose à lever lourdes calendes où dort un quidam sous une pierre écrite pour ainsi dire tombale rouge à l'intérieur où grouille une vermine pendant que violet dans sa nuit l'épi du maïs dort ouvert moi la bougie du sommeil éteint la langue retournée au ventre pour dormir à la fin entre les reins langue morte couchée là sur cailloux bleus de toute sa vie longue où boit le futur qui meurt aux éclats car mort c'est illettré et nu dans la maison de cent mille vers où ne parle plus le chiendent mais regarde l'œil noir de la suie. . . . .

*

Légumes cuits langue farcie j'ai le rêve impossible de parler cru les fourmis noyées du sens dans l'eau sale d'une cuisine où l'arrière-goût prend à la gorge et me voilà par effraction dans la maison maternelle où j'ai parlé ventriloque me voilà voler la langue où s'abouchait le père et brûler les bibles en allumant leurs dessous roses. . . . .

*

Le ciel est alors marchepied du gouffre où tremble le sang où résonne entre les tempes la migraine battue sur la falaise de l'os mais le rire secouant le crâne c'est la nouvelle amoureuse elle balaie devant ma porte autruche dont j'enlève les falbalas puis je l'envole en camisole de noces. . . . .

*

La vue première de l'œil natal retourné sous la robe un festin de larmes et dix mille jours attablés qui roulaient sous la dent creuse du ciel mais sur la prairie demandez-vous mais c'était la chaise vide attendant que s'assoie la mort nuageuse on aurait dit le ventre empaillé de la mère litière où j'ai vu flamber les poissons du sang (battu dans la boue un homme en neige digérait l'animelle lente-ment coulée du crâne ce caillou retourné noir dans le poumon d'un dieu mort dont le chiendent grimpait au ventre et si lourde levait la langue tombale tuile rose de la maison maternelle où le rêve en arrière parlait créole. . . . .

*

38

A pink tongue for raising weighty calends where a john doe sleeps beneath a written stone a gravestone so to speak red on the inside crawling with some vermin while the corn cob violet in its night sleeps open for me sleep's candle snuffs out the tongue turned back to the belly to sleep at last within the loins dead tongue lying there on blue pebbles of your whole long life where the future drinks dying in blasts for dead is illiterate and naked in the house of a thousand million worms or verses where the couch-grass no longer speaks but gazes at the black eye of soot. . . . .

*

Cooked vegetables stuffed tongue I dream the impossible dream of speaking raw the drowned ants of sense in dirty cooking water with an after-taste that catches in the throat and there I am breaking into my mother's house where I spoke like a ventriloquist there I am stealing the tongue where the father got his mouth and burning the bibles by lighting their pink underbellies. . . . .

*

The sky is then the running-board of the abyss where blood trembles where the migraine beaten on the bone's cliff resounds in the temples but laughter shakes the skull this is the new admirer she sweeps my doorstep like an ostrich I pluck her plumes and then fly her away in a bridal camisole. . . . .

*

The first sight of the eye of my birth upturned under the dress a feast of tears and ten thousand days at a table days rolling under the hollow tooth of the heavens but surely on the meadow you ask and yet it was the empty chair waiting for cloudy death to sit down you might have thought it was the stuffed belly of the mother litter in which I saw fish alight swimming in blood (beaten in the mud a snow man was digesting sweatbreads gently flowing from the skull that upturned black pebble in the lung of a dead god whose couch-grass was climbing over his belly and lifted the gravestone tongue so heavy pink tile of the mother's house where the backwards dream spoke creole. . . . .

*

Une grenouille volubile ventre ouvert au soir parle au fond de moi
en épelant mes organes dans sa langue de veuve elle mange la prairie
sachant qu'en langue vive au verbe ignoré organe se dit poisson
lune gonflé par la mort le ciel devient alors plaisir du sens autre-
ment dit la saoulographie des rouges gorges et l'animal rouge en-
cornant la nuit s'entend comme coqueluche. . . . .

*

Quant à dire dromadaire de la soif c'est langue cruelle quand les
corps bossus vident leur eau car la mémoire c'est le frein de ce
premier moment divisé depuis en saisons du zodiaque a l'entrée le
bord de la folie et derrière les portes d'éléphant un vieillard sur
violoncelle disant mes engelures mésange lyre mes anges lourds
mes injures et craignant mise à mort . . . .

*

Les tiroirs de ma tête ouverts ils étalent une valse de vieux linges
et déguisements les tiroirs de ma tête où sont rangées plusieurs
nuits sont l'escalier de quatre douleurs descendu huit à huit par
les épingles à chapeau tombant d'un grenier où une fille écorchée
à cause d'un lapin qui refuse la saignée demande l'impossible à
propos de la pluie (la voilà la pluie les étoiles pissent de peur une
aveugle boit ma nuit longtemps confite en moi dans sa gorge se
noient les rats mangeurs de mes yeux ils y voyaient l'ordure dans
le blanc les salauds . . . .

*

Cancer du sens couvant ses œufs noirs sous mille métaphores de
l'amour un crapaud bavard mange mes organes en épelant les mots
de la langue veuve et pour le plaisir du sens la mort aussi grosse
que le bœuf encorne la nuit (retournée dans ma bouche la mort
mâche mes régions natales repas de la mémoire au fond des larmes
la dernière aube attablée sous la carie du ciel la voûte éclairée noire
d'un porche ici là ouvrant le phalanstère des proies ou joie anthro-
pophage dans un tombeau d'araignées où se tissent les mots. . . . . .

*

40

A voluble frog belly open to the evening speaks in the depths of me spelling out my organs in its widow's language it eats the meadow knowing that in living language of unknown word organ is called moon fish swollen by death then the heavens become the pleasure of sense in other words red-breast booze-up and the red animal goring the night sounds like whooping cough. . . . .

*

As for saying dromedary of thirst it's a cruel tongue when humped bodies empty their waters for memory puts the break on that initial movement divided since into the seasons of the zodiac the edge of madness at the entry and behind the elephant doors an old man on a cello speaking my chilblains my angelic titmice reading my lyre my heavy angels my insults and fearing execution. . . . .

*

The drawers of my head are open displaying a waltz of old linen and disguises the drawers of my head where several nights are put away are the stairs of four sorrows run down eight at a time by the hatpins tumbling from a loft where a girl flayed because of a rabbit's refusal to be bled asks the impossible of the rain (here comes the rain the stars piss with fear a blind woman drinks my night long since crystallised within me in her throat the rats drown which would eat my eyes they saw the filth in the whites of them the bastards. . . . .

*

Cancer of sense hatching its black eggs beneath a thousand metaphors of love a garrulous toad eats my organs spelling out the words of the widower tongue and for the pleasure of sense death huge as a bullock gores the night (upturned in my mouth death masticates the regions where I was born a meal of memory in the depth of tears the last dawn at the table under the caries of the heavens the black lit vault of a porch here and there opening the phalanstery of preys or cannibal play in a spiders' tomb where the web of words is woven. . . . .

*

Et sur la prairie la mère vidée par les poissons du sang on aurait dit chaise dépaillée litière où j'ai vu flamber la mort nuageuse digérant le caillou lentement coulé du crâne et l'animelle enroulée dans le poumon d'un dieu mort (dans son ventre tombal la langue est maternelle. . . . .

*

Licorne levée dans le lit de la mère ta chair j'en viens j'y retourne et je me couche à la fin dans la forêt parricide du cerveau mais là dans la caboche brûlée un combat de coqs n'en finit pas qu'on ouvre le cirque de lumière et tant pis que je me voie couché sur la décharge de plumes. . . . .

*

Ou sur le galimatias d'où je viens ce sera le retour de la colère à poings fermés dans le ventre où je buvais la pluie retour de la rage que j'ai voulue volubile comme la mort et bête à manger l'alphabet battu blanc de l'aïeule illettrée . . . .

*

Au moment de mourir je laisserai la main dans le livre des vieux mots la main refermée sur les moineaux mobiles accouplés depuis toujours dans la volière de mon crâne au ciel souterrain les moineaux retournés à la chair qui roucouleront le sens dont le baiser me lèche mais les moineaux je les entends comme alouette ou miroir aux mouettes alors revient la peur de mille mensonges en si peu de mots seraient-ils les seuls moteurs de l'horloge. . . . .

*

L'horloge à marée haute engrossée du déluge c'est elle qui parle et sa mort torrentielle qui lave mes paroles c'est donc sa méduse qui me lèche (et qui laisse un ciel si cru l'illusion de le mordre pourtant ce n'est pas l'appétit du songe en moi plutôt le désir de trente-six dessous mais le ciel est partout comme un œil bleu où le soleil saigne à blanc vulgaire sablier du sang (et ma tête un iceberg de mille ans où sont pris les poissons céphalés. . . . .

*

And on the meadow the mother emptied out by the fish in her blood like a chair with its straw coming out a litter where I saw a milky death flame and digest the pebble dripped slowly from the skull and the sweatbread rolled in the lung of a dead god (in his grave-yard belly the tongue is maternal. . . . .

*

Unicorn sitting up in the bed of the mother your flesh I come from there I return there and at last lie down in the parricide forest of the brain but there in the burnt bonce a cockfight goes on for ever let the circus of light be opened and too bad if I see myself lying on a dump of the feathers. . . . .

*

Or on the gibberish I come from this will be the return of hard-fisted anger in the belly where I drank the rain return of the rage I wanted voluble as death and stupid enough to eat the illiterate grandmother's alphabet beaten blank. . . . .

*

At the moment of death I shall leave my hand in the book of old words hand closed on the sparky sparrows coupled since forever in the bird-house of my cranium with the underground sky the sparrows returned to the flesh will warble sense whose kiss is tonguing me but I sense them as a lark or a mirage of gulls so then returns the fear of a thousand lies in so few words could they be the only movers of the clock. . . . .

*

The clock at high tide pregnant with the flood is the one that speaks and its torrential death washes my words and so it's the clock's medusa licking me (and which leaves behind such a raw sky still the illusion of biting it doesn't come from a taste for dream within me rather a desire for thirty-six below but the sky is everywhere like a blue eye where the sun bleeds an ordinary hourglass white with blood for sand (and my head an iceberg a thousand years old the cephalate fish captured inside. . . . .

*

III

Dans les mines prolifères du mental j'ai trouvé le ciel ouvert où
bourdonne une abeille comme un nom jamais butiné portant l'écho
de la mort étrangère dans la bouche d'autrui devenue death mais
dans nos monuments de siècles au nombre de quarante ou plus je
me promène en burnou sans cacher la lettre morte à mon front
(mensonge monumental à parler des profondeurs où brille l'absence
de l'or une pelle à charbon pour fronde du rien car dans le canyon
creusé de la conversation la pierre qui roule au delta tricéphale n'est
qu'un mot supplémentaire sur l'idiome de la mort. . . . .

*

Empire inca écroulé dans le peu de bruit dans la mémoire du noyau
troué d'une cerise introuvable comme si le verrou doucement tourné
de la phrase ouvrait à l'œil du voyeur un champ labouré par l'anté-
diluvien (la maison mère à l'écoute d'un ciel sourd où l'on vend à
la criée l'article de la mort tombé dans l'oreille d'abord ourlée de
bave et du verbe végétal (les miettes d'un nom aboli à le marteler
dans le cœur comble et continu de la foison un cœur anthracite
l'avale carnivore et c'est un bruit de fougères et de mâchoires dans
le temple vide la chambre de plein vent. . . . .

*

En météore enflé de noyaux reproduits retombera l'histoire perdue
de Méloé l'œil de l'abeille sur la mort vieillie d'années-lumière dans
le jardin d'anciennes nominations soulevé par l'écœurement de la
parole sa dentelle de pourriture ouvrant un cœur encore vert (dans
le livre défait dieu métaphore de la mémoire baiserait diane fille
mère enfin nue dans le drap du poème où se livre le vent . . . . . .

*

III

In the rich mines of the mind I found the open heavens where a bee buzzes like a name never gathered carrying the echo of foreign death to the mouths of others where it's now mort but in our monuments to the centuries numbering forty or more I walk along in a burnous the dead letter on my forehead plain to see (monumental lie to speak of the depths where the absence of gold glitters a coal shovel for a sling at the void for in the deep-dug canyon of conversation the stone rolling to the tricephalous delta is but a word added to the idiom of death. . . . .

*

Inca empire crumbled in amongst the slight noise in the memory of the pierced kernel of an undiscoverable cherry as though the bolt of the sentence gently turned opened the voyeur's eye to a field tilled by the antediluvian (the mother-house listening for deaf heavens where there's an auction of the article of death fallen on an ear edged at first with slobber and the vegetal verb (the crumbs of a name abolished hammered away in the heart of abundance bursting and continuing an anthracite heart carnivorously swallows it and there is a noise of ferns and jaws in the empty temple the chamber full of wind. . . . .

*

Like a meteor swollen with reproduced kernels the lost story of Meloe will fall the eye of the bee on death aged by light-years in the garden of ancient namings brought up by the nausea of the word its lace of rot opening up a heart still green (in the unmade book god the metaphor of memory would sleep with diana child mother finally naked in the sheet of the poem where the wind lets go. . . .

*

L'image raturée d'un rongeur sur champ de tournesols comme la rature fière de rayer l'or rongerait le mot soleil les mots du poème sont mille lapins multipliés couvrant la terre de leur poil jusqu'au ventre bleu de la mer et là tournant de l'œil pour voir l'icare retombé dans l'à jamais des catastrophes jamais content du vol et recommençant jusqu'à la casse . . . .

*

Mots dans les mots momifiés où s'enferme le voleur dans un louvre pour la nuit champollion d'une pyramide inutile sauf à réveiller les papillons millénaires sans origine sinon leur mort (louvre mais parlement sans loi parlemensonge imprimé jamais pareil dans les nuages noués les mouchoirs de dieu perdant la mémoire. . . . .

*

De l'os dans l'oreille de l'égypte au caillou bouchant les menstrues le nil n'est pas loin ni la paille des ventres crocodiles et mot à mot le livre modifié mars au commencement le poème recommence dans la bouche maternelle sept filles de la mémoire à venir (parlerie de bastille en désert où passent les pharaons la pierre au cou du haut d'étretat mes suicides mille fois répétés le sang dans la baignoire d'un cœur vraiment levé raymond roussel voyant sa vie va dégueuler. . . . .

*

Sous la maison du phraseur s'ouvre un champ de mars peuplé de souffleurs (elle sous une ombrelle vers le jardin d'hiver la mère à gauche de la mémoire adam aux antipodes dans un fossile du lutétien et bien avant la parole grouille au cœur du sophora (des jeudis entiers à balbutier dans la serre innommable des grammaires parmi les mots plantés là par les révérends pères voyageurs ou buffon parvenu. . . . .

*

The scratched out image of a rodent on a field of sunflowers like the scratching out proud of scoring gold would gnaw the word sun the words of the poem are a thousand multiplying rabbits covering the earth with their pelt up to the blue belly of the sea and fainting there to see the icarus fallen into the forever of catastrophes never happy with flight and starting over to the point of scrap. . . . .

*

Words in the mummified words where the thief locks himself in a louvre for the night champollion of a pyramid of no use if not to wake the millennial butterflies with no origin but their death (louvre but lawless parliament printed parliamendacity unparalleled in the knotted clouds the handkerchiefs of god losing his memory. . . . . .

*

From the bone in egypt's ear to the pebble blocking the menstrual flow the nile is never far nor the straw of the crocodile bellies and word for word the modified book march at the beginning the poem begins once more in the maternal mouth seven daughters of the memory to come (bastille talking-shop in the desert where the pharaohs pass with a stone round their necks from the height of étretat my suicides are repeated a thousand times blood in the bathtub of a heart truly raised raymond roussel throws up at the sight of his life. . . . .

*

Below the phrasemonger's house opens a march field crowded with prompters (she beneath a parasol near the winter garden the mother on the left of memory adam in the antipodes in a lutetian fossil and well before speech swarms in the heart of the sophora (whole days off spent stammering in the unnameable hothouse of grammars and words left there by exploring reverend fathers or an upstart buffoon. . . . .

*

Plus loin des bernardins pétrifiés des fontaines à paroles urinant encore dans le vase de la langue la botanique d'un auteur enterré juif sous le jardin des plantes (labrunie baisé par la reine à la fin c'est nerval vomissant sa langue et qui souffle leur mort aux parleurs de châtelet son corps dans le champ retourné grammaire à la craie l'archet sur les nerfs il nous écrit parfois . . . .

*

Oreille ma prison d'enclumes à l'entrée du corps ce marteau couché rouge dans une chambre à sélinonte jamais la même où dort un tyran (si la chambre de l'œil est mouillée c'est un cerf il n'y a qu'un mâle pour pisser) repose dans la tombe d'un mauvais dionysos dont la pourriture monte encore dans ces contrées (du mobilier de torture la table de calcaire est à deux mètres plus bas sur elle de chambre en chambre un siècle avant pierre larousse écrivait. . . . .

*

L'utopie ce géranium à l'orient des grammaires bourdonne des seules mouches venues de sodome l'envers écrit de leur mort sous un ciel caillé d'étoiles (dans le jardin des langues au fond d'une allée manque un château propriétaire comme du ciel metro goldwyn mayer se prenant pour noé mais les langues mammifères et les mammouths ont fait leur temps c'est d'un corps sans organe que fourier parle aujourd'hui. . . . .

*

Ma sœur liseuse d'aigle sa voix d'orthophoniste à prononcer les morts qu'on change au panthéon le coffre aux tiroirs écrits dans le jardin de geneviève (le tourment de stéphane qui se prend pour lui disait-elle il goûterait bien l'aphasie pour le plaisir de répéter crénom jusqu'à sa mort en cassant la machine bègue où bute le symbole (poème déjà périmé à lire comme on lit magyar posta dans un album deux mots étrangers pourtant quelque part d'une langue officielle tatouée de tampons (ah la hache sidérale d'un lecteur à quatre mains pour que saignent encore bleus ces vieux papiers dans les halles abattues bâtissez bibliothèques avec odeurs d'épluchures . . . .

Further on petrified cistercians fountains of words still urinating in the vase of language the botany of an author buried jewish beneath the botanical gardens (labrunie kissed by the queen in the end it's nerval vomiting his tongue and prompting death to the chatterers in the fort his body in the turned over soil grammar on the board in chalk a bow stroking his nerves he writes to us sometimes. . . .

*

Ear my anvil prison at the entrance to my body that hammer lying red-hot in a chamber in syracuse never the one where a tyrant sleeps (if the eye's chamber is wet it's a stag none pisses like a male) is at rest in the tomb of a bad dionysus whose rot still rises in these regions (in the furniture of torture the limestone table is two metres further down on that very one a century before from room to room pierre larousse would write. . . . .

*

Utopia that geranium in the orient of grammars buzzes with the only flies to come from sodom the written reverse of their death under a sky clotted with stars (in the garden of languages at the end of an avenue a proprietorial chateau is missing like metro goldwyn mayer sky taking itself for noah but the mammalian tongues and the mammoths have done their time nowadays fourier talks from a body with no organ . . . .

*

My sister eagle-eyed reader her speech-therapist's voice just right for uttering the dead changed in the pantheon the chest of written drawers in the garden of genevieve (the torment of stephen who thinks it's him she would say he'd certainly enjoy aphasia for the pleasure of repeating damn and blast to his dying moment smashing the stammering machine and the symbol trips over it (a poem already out of date read like magyar posta two foreign words in a stamp album but still belonging to some part of an official language all tattooed with rubber franking marks (ah the sidereal axe of a four-handed reader still being bled blue blood by those old papers in the knackered market halls build libraries smelling of potato peel. . . .

IV

Corps l'écriture braille la machine aveugle et sourde malabaraise à
broyer les paroles un os de rat dans le talon (un café d'étoiles moulu
dans les reins des veuves salivent dans le marc le rien de la parole
ou pur anagramme de la mort. . . . .

*

Outre l'écriture le peigne chiné rouge dans le chignon des nuits la
chute des comètes file un sens italique où *la treizième revient* (la roue
les questions le corps roué sur un billard démeublé d'un forain
céleste au ciel chinois toujours un lundi s'en va. . . . .

*

Des fraises écrasées sur le sol où tombe le ciel ce météorite d'orgueil
ramassées dans les chiffons de deux mille pages à venir (l'éléphant
du lutétien déterré porcelaine de la patience ne priez plus pour
nous la bibliothèque bouge où les champignons mangent à table
avec les arcadiens de la forêt (de la fleur à la fleur d'un pollen à
l'autre un œuf est demeuré parfois vide . . . .

*

Une langue nouvelle ces flatteurs hiéroglyphes pour un nettoyeur
de cadavres la poule des pharaons les mêmes dix fois maudits la
mort du premier né avant l'obscurité mais le papier des fables pâlit
d'un ponge ancien lu à la loupe. . . . .

*

Éphèse à sept sommeils de la bretagne *an ifern yen* au pays du
père où l'enfer est froid lavandières de la nuit tordez mon linge à
l'envers le lit des voueuses et la moitié sinistre du livre au firma-
ment refermé de ma mort à proprement parler. . . . .

*

IV

Body writing yells braille the blind deaf and beefy word-crushing machine a rat's bone in the heel (a coffee made of stars ground in the loins widows are salivating in the dregs the void of the word or pure anagram of death. . . . .

*

Besides writing the comb dyed red in the chignon of nights the comets' fall threads an italic sense where *the thirteenth returns* (the wheel the questions the body broken on the dilapidated billiard table of a celestial fairground artist with a chinese backdrop always on a monday he'll push off. . . . .

*

Strawberries crushed on the earth where the sky falls that meteorite of pride are gathered in the rags of two thousand pages to come (elephant of the unearthed lutetian porcelain of patience pray no longer for us the library moves where the mushrooms eat at a table with the sylvan arcadians (from flower to flower from one pollen to the other an egg sometimes stayed empty. . . . .

*

These flattering hieroglyphs a new language for a cleaner of corpses the ten times accursed pharaohs and their wenches the death of the first born before dark but the paper of fables pales in an ancient francis ponge read through a glass . . . .

*

Ephesus seven sleeps away from Brittany *an ifern yen* in the land of the father where hell freezes washerwomen of the night wring my linen inside out the bed of the vow-takers and the sinister half of the book with the closed firmament of my death strictly speaking. . . .

*

Aloès amertume armoise avortement balsamine impatience d'une messe à l'envers et voyelles des voueuses dans les consonnes de l'anaon comme cyprès deuil et débauche hortensia froideur mais menthe chaleur passionnelle quand un retour de sens attise le château alors mouron rendez-vous sous les orties de l'érotisme (et la malherbe ruminée. . . . .

*

Chercheurs de pain à quoi bon la neige et l'orpiment quand les mots sont en miettes dans la bouche à dévorer l'assassin d'hortense en abyssinie sur le fumier du porc le plus froid la mort vêtue de soie parle l'ostiaque à dix-sept ans la mort sara d'une sœur de parole. . .

*

De chou en cyclamen à promener nos maladies parmi les plantes l'hiver passé le fumier brûle et les vieilles vérités comme violettes à bouillir et sangsues sur l'anus (des compresses d'oignons cuits sur les mots cette mort dans le livre à répéter garamond. . . . .

*

. . . . un planétarium où le père illettré nous délivre du sens et de l'inceste nos phrases incisées (raturées rouges sous le siège de ma mère cardinale des ourses tombent de langue muette en syllabes à marier l'autre langue trois phrases commencées dans le jardin des mégalithes et l'incongru de chouette en cyclope (menuisier seul tu saurais le dernier mot mais la cheville est inutile à l'œil fermé sans toi la main gauche sous la paupière enfonce l'ongle dans l'abcès du pléonasme. . . . .

*

Château clochard j'écrivais *de visu* le château mallarmé dans la mémoire (la rainette ruminée les bovins rêvent un ver dans le fruit de ma tête le rêve à l'imparfait dans l'éléphant d'étretat les portes de craie montrent tout (le crottin de l'éden ou nulle part. . . . . . .

*

Aloe acrid artemisia abortion balsam impatience of an upturned mass and vowels of the vow-takers in the consonants of the soul like cypress mourning and hortensia debauchery coldness but mint heat of the passions when a return of sense fans the flame of the château then scarlet pimpernel meeting under the nettles of eroticism (and the remasticated plumbago. . . . .

*

Seekers of bread what use snow and orpiment when words crumble in the mouth set to devour the assassin from hortensia to abyssinia on the dung of the coldest swine death dressed in silk speaks the lingo of ostia at seventeen the african death of a word sister. . . . . .

*

From cabbage to cyclamen last winter as we walked our maladies amongst the plants the dung burns and the old verities like violets to be boiled and leeches on the anus (compresses of cooked onion on the words a death in the book to be done over in garamond. . .

*

. . . . a planetarium where the illiterate father frees us from sense and incest our incised sentences (scratched out in red beneath the seat of my cardinal mother bears fall from a mute tongue into syllables to be married off the other tongue three sentences begun in the garden of the megaliths and in incongruity of screech-owl into cyclops (carpenter you alone would know the last word but the peg is useless to the closed eye without you the left hand beneath the eyelid sinks a fingernail into the abscess of pleonasm. . . . .

*

Hobo castle I wrote *de visu* the mallarmé castle into my memory (the rennet once remasticated the bovine dream a worm in the fruit that is my head dream in the imperfect inside the elephant of étretat the chalk gates show all (the droppings of eden or nowhere. . .

*

Sur le fraîche ancien le bruit des brouilles familiales ma langue en friche où ramasser les mots dans le patois du père robinson bien sûr mais quel vendredi pour conjuguer le temps toujours à compter d'aujourd'hui moins les rognures d'hier ces quartiers de phrase d'une boucherie lunatique (lecteur quel vendredi fait-il quand le sens n'est plus férié sablier pour temps d'hiver cadran pour temps solaire et le couple mirage/oasis qui parle l'hébreu. . . . .

*

Dictionnaire la boutique bavarde des morts lui manqueraient les mots de méricourt et la veine de la parole entre la falaise et l'éléphant recto/verso (au bord des mots comme à des balcons d'hlm sèche une mer morte la morve de la langue à remanger (ostiaque et mort parlé les langues se mangent froid dans la parole creuse où les corps ont conservé nos manies troglodytes. . . . .

*

Éléonore compostelle pérégrine vers nulle part où la nommer vers nul mausolée de saint jacques ou lénine même à main gauche du labyrinthe où s'ouvrent les guillemets sur les latrines de l'orthographe et la propriété des dahlias (meurt le minotaure dans la grammaire de monique ce corps qui pourrissait comme lapsus. . . . .

*

La main gauche qui n'écrit pas la main de mon mort biographe et le membre du père la même atrophie dans le trou d'une mémoire longtemps retenue comme l'étron de l'éléphant nocturne et labiales dehors une grande ourse de prose (les galaxies d'initiales ne bégaient plus dans les palaces de déraison trop villas pour être vrais des vélos roulent vers prairial aux dimanches bigames. . . . .

*

On the old unmowed meadow the noise of family feuds my fallow
tongue gathering the words in the patois of old father robinson of
course but where's friday to conjugate our time always today minus
the erosions of yesterday those hunks of sentences from a lunatic
butcher (reader which friday is it when sense isn't a day off any more
hourglass for winter time sun-dial for solar time and the mirage/
oasis couple speaking hebrew. . . . .

*

Dictionary chatter-shop of the dead the words of méricourt would
be missing and the vein of speech on both sides between the cliff
and the elephant (on the edge of words as on council-flat balconies
a dead sea is hung out to dry tongue-snot for future remastication
(ostiac and the dead man spoken languages are served cold in the
hollow word where bodies have preserved our troglodyte manias. . .

*

Eleanor compostella peregrines nowhere to name her in no saint
james or lenin mausoleum or even on the left in the labyrinth
where the inverted commas open the latrines of spelling and the
dahlias' property (dies the minotaur in the grammar of monica
that body that was rotting like a lapsus. . . . .

*

Left hand not writing the hand of my dummy the biographer and my
father's member the same atrophy in the black hole of a memory
long retained like the night elephant's turd and labials on the out-
side a great bear of prose (the galaxies of initials no longer stammer
in the grand hotels of unreason too much like villas for verity bikes
ride up to the month of prairial and its bigamous sundays. . . . . .

*

V

Après solaise et vernaison vienne venise à s'enfoncer dans les mots
le maure sonnant l'heure et la mort marchandise dans nos draps le
noir sous la cerisaie *made in japan* (jetés du boudoir céleste et
couronnés par l'œillet du choléra le cœur chauve dans le jardin
maraîcher (tête-bêche le corps démembré d'osiris mangé par les
cellules mères mortelles veuf et volage mangé vivant dans un repas
gelé (la vierge au marteau frappait le champagne banquet perpétuel
dans la maison des nombrils le sang craché devant la porte (...)
volubilis coupé l'anacoluthe à l'origine qui bâille après poème un
prénom goinfre craché par jonas quarante jours dans blanche neige
sept nains branleurs de baleine dont poucet sucé jusqu'à l'os dans
le ventre de mars ils prénomment la mort coupée des majuscules
biographes de leur main morte à l'état civil écrivant le prénom vice
versa dans la chambre plurielle si les gardiens de la phrase pouvaient
mourir sous minuscule (listes et lettrines la morgue est pleine des
post-scriptum même pas suppléments d'un livre à reliure de chagrin
où finnegans n'en finit pas (mais les conversations de café tabac les
taire est trahison de roturière mythologie les harengs saurs sous la
pluie furent mes seules sirènes la mort un sale dispensaire dans la
rue des poissonniers. . . . .

V

After solaise and vernaison let venice come and dig deep in words
the moor sounding the hour and death moneyed in our sheets
darkness under the cherry orchard *made in japan* (thrown from the
celestial boudoir and crowned by the carnation of cholera a bald
heart in the cottage garden (top-to-tail the dismembered body of
osiris eaten widowed and whimsical by the mortal mother cells
devoured white-hot in a frozen feast (the virgin and hammer was
raining blows on the champagne perpetual banquet in the house
of navels blood belched in front of the door (. . .) cut convulvulus
anacoluthon in the beginning that yawns after poem a gluttonous
forename belched out by jonah forty days in snow white seven
dwarfs whale wankers and tom thumb sucked to the bone in the
belly of mars they forename death cut from biographers' capital
letters in a hand dead to the registry writing the forename vice-
versa in the plural chamber if the guardians of the sentence could
die in lower case (lists and letter-heads the morgue is full of post-
scripts not even supplements to a book bound in chagrin where
finnegans goes on and on (but the café conversations to silence
them is betrayal of vulgar mythology smoked herrings in the rain
were my only sirens death a dirty dispensary in fish lane. . . . . .

Les balcons de Babel

The Balconies of Babel

(1977)

À une aïeule illettrée

To an illiterate grandmother

Le théâtre est bien réel, au nord éloigné d'un jardin où l'on a réuni les espèces végétales les plus rares: Assuérus, Auréa, Catinat, Alice et Céleste, Cordélia, Clématis, Orion, Sirius et Cassiopée, Opéra, Châtelet, Crépuscule, Mentor et Spectabilis sont les héroïnes en pleine terre de ce théâtre naturel. Un sophora rapporté par un voyageur désœuvré, un prunus qui fleurit en avril, un arbre mâle et centenaire sont avec la maison de Cuvier, les serres tropicales, le jardin d'hiver et le petit labyrinthe, le vivarium à main gauche de l'éléphant de mer, les autres stations de cette promenade pour dieux minuscules, qui croient serrer le monde dans un mouchoir comme ils tiennent un dictionnaire dans leur main; ici, c'est le jardin des nominations sous le ciel, dont les constellations trois à trois sont des miroirs tournants, qui nous montrent tour à tour, mais jamais dans le même ordre, les empreintes de nos rêves: la tête le père le cheval   le vent les bois le coq ébouriffé   la lune l'oreille le porc   le nain la nourriture la mère   le tonnerre l'œil le faisan   le lac la bouche la concubine   le fou le souffleur le pendu

Au fond de cet espace cartographié, un bâtiment délabré fut successivement palais religieux, bibliothèque et muséum; aujourd'hui, c'est un théâtre dont la façade est muette, sauf une inscription dont quelques lettres sont encore lisibles:

M   M   S   OI   ELLE

Selon son goût, on peut compléter ainsi l'inscription mutilée: muséum d'histoire naturelle, ou monument des lois universelles. Pour ma part, je n'ai jamais pu décider entre ces deux interprétations: aucune lecture n'est vraie, quand il s'agit de lire aussi les mots entre les mots.

Dans l'encadrement d'une fenêtre, la nature personnifiée tient un livre de pierre, qu'elle semble donner à lire à la statue de Buffon: un oiseau mort dans la main gauche, la tête penchée et lasse, il est le souffleur pétrifié de ce théâtre à ciel ouvert.

*

The theatre is quite real, to the distant North of a garden where the rarest of botanical species have been gathered: Assuerus, Aurea, Catinat, Alice and Celeste, Cordelia, Clematis, Orion, Sirius and Cassiopeia, Opera, Chatelet, Crépuscule, Mentor and Spectabilis are the firmly embedded heroines of this natural theatre. A sophora brought back by an idle traveller, a prune tree flowering in April, a male tree a hundred years old all with Cuvier's house, the tropical hothouses, the winter garden and the little labyrinth, the vivarium of the sea-elephant on the left, the other stopping places on this walk for tiny giants who think to enclose the world in a pocket-handkerchief as they would hold a dictionary in their hand; here we are in the garden of nomination beneath the heavens, whose three by three constellations are revolving mirrors showing in turn, but never in the same order, the imprints of our dreams: the head the father the horse   the wind the woods the ruffled cock   the moon the ear the pig   the dwarf the food the mother   thunder the eye the pheasant   the lake the mouth the concubine   the joker the prompter the hanged man

At the back of this space mapped out, a dilapidated building was in turn a religious palace, a library and a museum; today it is a theatre with a blank facade apart from an inscription where some letters are still legible:

M   M   S   OI   ELLE

The mutilated inscription can be completed in different ways according to taste: Museum of Natural History or Monument to Universal Law. Personally I have never been able to choose between these two interpretations: no reading is true when words are read between words.

In the frame of a window, a personification of Nature is holding a book in stone which she seems to be giving to the statue of Buffon to read: a dead bird in his left hand, head weary and bowed, he is the petrified prompter in this theatre open to the heavens.

*

On entre côté cour (orties blanches et poules accroupies, et derrière le théâtre il y a les bois...) ou côté suicide dont une nonne aux yeux bleus garde l'entrée (une voûte antédiluvienne soutenue par deux ossements, moitiés de mâchoire d'un monstre marin).

La seule plante qui n'ait pas de nom marqué produit des fruits étranges, des baies violettes et amères que la nonne vous fait avaler afin que vous perdiez en partie mémoire et langage: les bouches de savoir sont des bouches de chagrin, et raconter est un mensonge impossible (dans la boutique de l'embaumeur *è vietato bestemmiare*, il est interdit de blasphémer).

La bibliothèque a brûlée sous la révolution, il en reste des ruines à côté du columbarium, où des personnages ont laissé leurs noms sur des centaines d'alvéoles: Rose Galles, Séverine Perruquet, Eva Corneil, Maurice Varin athée vétéran... c'est la mort qui chante ici l'air du catalogue.

À la hauteur du premier étage, un promenoir est fleuri de géraniums et d'œillets nains; de ce balcon funèbre on aperçoit au loin le lavoir où l'enfant naturel vient prononcer son nom de famille avant la mue complète de sa voix, pendant que la grand-mère tire d'une lessiveuse, au bout d'un bâton, des draps de lit fumants, des serviettes et des nappes «nids d'abeilles» brodées d'initiales. Elle rince le linge plusieurs fois, pour le laver de ses souvenirs véniels et de ses secrets.

Des vieillards, qui jouent aux échecs sur des chaises de jardin, déplacent lentement des pièces rouges et noires (devant le cadran solaire, un maître dc jeu change au fur et a mesure la position de personnages «grandeur nature», sur un damier de sable rose et gris). Seule la pluie qu'ils ne cessent d'espérer pourrait interrompre leur partie; l'enjeu en est une veuve d'ivoire qui n'a jamais appartenu à personne, une folle qui les regarde en parlant sous elle, et deviner ce qu'elle dit pourrait occuper jusqu'au déluge.

À défaut de comprendre ses romans, on sacrifie à ses pieds la taupe mâle ou licorne vulgaire des jardins, quand elle sort de son trou pour manger des touffes d'oseille. On met ensuite sa peau à sécher avec celle des lapins, pendus dans le clapier, derrière le pardessus qui les cache.

*

You go in front right (white nettles and squatting hens, and behind the theatre are the woods...) or up left, the suicide way, where a blue-eyed nun minds the entrance (an antediluvian vault supported by two large bones, the two jaws of some sea-monster).

The only plant without a name produces a strange fruit, bitter violet berries that the nun makes you swallow so that you lose speech and memory in part: the mouths of knowledge are mouths of chagrin, and telling stories is an impossible lie (in the embalmer's shop *è vietato bestemmiare*, no blaspheming).

The library burned down during the revolution, a few ruins remain by the side of the columbarium where important figures have left their names on hundreds of cells: Rose Galles, Séverine Perruquet, Eva Corneil, Maurice Varin the veteran atheist...here death sings the tune of the catalogue.

At first floor level, there is a walkway with flowering geraniums and dwarf carnations: from this funereal balcony the wash-house can be seen in the distance where the illegitimate child comes to utter his family name before his voice breaks completely, while the grandmother pulls from a wash-tub, on the end of a stick, steaming sheets, towels, and honeycomb stitched tablecloths with embroidered initials. She rinses the linen several times to wash it clean of its venial memories and its secrets.

Old men playing chess on garden chairs slowly move red and black chessmen (in front of the sundial, a master of ceremonies changes the position of "life-size figures" as the game proceeds on a board of pink and grey sand). Only the rain which they hope for endlessly could interrupt their game; they are playing for an ivory widow who has never belonged to anyone, a madwoman watching them who talks in her pants, and guessing what she says could take until the flood.

For want of understanding her tall stories, the male mole or the common garden unicorn is sacrificed at her feet when she comes out of her hole to eat bunches of sorrel. Its skin is then put out to dry with the rabbit skins, hung in the hutch behind the overcoat that keeps them from view.

*

De la partie fermée du théâtre vient une voix qui répète pour elle seule son monologue insensé.

Ce qu'elle dissimule n'est pas de l'ordre du récit, bien que je ne cherche à rien cacher; mais ma fatigue est parfois si lourde que j'ai l'impression de tomber dans mon propre corps, la demeure profonde et bleue où le théâtre est tendu d'un voile de deuil, comme le trou du souffleur avant la représentation. Dans cette maison des morts, la voix «étranglée» serait-elle un rêve de pendaison?

Dans la même maison bleue l'aïeule est morte. Je suis arrivé trop tard le dernier soir: on venait de l'emporter, pour la ramener sans vie le lendemain. Je n'ai revu qu'un visage de cire, une figure de grévin que j'ai dû embrasser: dernier baiser, vulgaire à vomir, avant qu'on referme la boîte. Dans la cuisine, on a ouvert la huche et le grand buffet: le pain des morts aurait dû tomber en miettes entre nos mains. Plus tard, quatre déménageurs ont emporté la bière, et la maison est restée vide. Aujßourd'hui ce théâtre, entre le mort et le vif, le vrai et le faux, voudrait remplir l'espace, entrer dans le temps de la répétition. Certains soirs la relâche est forcée, à cause de mon haleine mauvaise: c'est mon ventre qui se vide comme celui de cette morte.

Mais je n'en ai pas fini avec mes maisons, mes espaces de somnambule. Au fond d'un corridor où couraient les rats (une vieille les étouffait sous ses pieds, elle restait des heures à attendre cette mort lente) s'ouvraient des pièces où j'ai vécu une enfance enfermée. Quand j'étais seul, j'entrais secrètement dans la chambre des parents. Derrière le lit, dans la pièce aux doubles rideaux toujours tirés, j'ai découvert un jour un seau sordide où trempaient des linges. Ensuite, j'ai soulevé le couvercle souvent, pour me voir dans ce miroir sale.

La même chambre était aussi l'espace rêvé du langage: c'est à la tête du lit qu'était rangé le seul livre de la maison, un vieux Larousse dont personne n'avait l'usage. Il fallait enjamber le lit (et le couvre-lit rouge) pour chercher pendant des heures le sens des mots interdits; pour feuilleter le livre en tremblant, avec la crainte d'être surpris dans cette position honteuse; pour embrasser à la première page la bouche de cette femme soufflant sur les mots, et qui semait leur sens à tous les vents de la peur.

From the closed part of the theatre comes a voice alone rehearsing its crazed monologue.

What it dissimulates is not part of any narrative, although I'm not trying to hide anything; but my weariness is sometimes so heavy that I sometimes feel I'm falling into my own body, the deep blue dwelling place where the theatre is draped in a funeral veil, like the prompter's box before a performance. In this house of the dead could the "strangled" voice be a dream of a hanging?

The grandmother had died in the same blue house. I arrived too late on the last evening: she had just been taken away, and her lifeless body was brought back the next day. All I saw was a waxen visage, a face out of Madame Tussaud's which I had to kiss: a last kiss, nauseatingly vulgar, before they closed the box. In the kitchen they opened the bread bin and the big sideboard: the bread of the dead should have fallen in crumbs from our hands. Later four stalwarts took away the bier, and the house remained empty for some time. Today this theatre, between the quick and the dead, the false and the true, would like to take the space over, find a way into rehearsal and time. Some nights the show has to be cancelled because of my bad breath: my belly emptying like the dead woman's.

But I haven't finished telling you about my houses, my sleep-walking spaces. At the end of a corridor running with rats (an old woman used to crush them to death under her feet, and spend hours watching that slow death) rooms would open out where I led a confined childhood. When I was alone I would go secretly into my parents' bedroom. Behind the bed, in this room with double curtains that were always drawn, one day I discovered a disgusting bucket where linen had been left to soak. Later I often lifted the lid to look at myself in that dirty mirror.

The same room was also the space of language I would dream of: the only book in the house was stowed away at the bed's head, an old Larousse for which no one had any use. You had to climb over the bed (and the red counterpane) to spend hours looking up forbidden words; leafing through the book with trembling hands, afraid of being caught in that shameful position; kissing the mouth of that woman on the first page who blows over the words and scatters their sense to all the winds of fear.

Depuis, les boiseries et les balcons de la chambre rouge sont tombés en poussière, et l'immeuble lépreux est démoli. C'est un champ de ruines entre le chemin des mères, la prairie de l'affût et la laiterie (on nomme ainsi le lieu de méditation, l'observatoire à ciel ouvert qui donne sur la voie lactée: les chambres où parfois le sang tourne en lait).

*

Au-delà commence la banlieue et ses villes vagues, murs manifestes et portes latentes. Les volets clos, le sommeil jusqu'à midi, et la forêt en lisière beaucoup plus loin: vers Presles et Saint-Leu, Nerville et Villiers-Adam. D'où l'on revenait en sueur, après s'être perdus – avec la peur et l'espoir de vieillir très vite.

Gennevilliers est à sept lieues, sans *postillons* ni *bêtes de songes*: nous n'allions jamais jusque là-bas. Mais l'Orient est à nos pieds, quand à la nuit tombante on surplombe les toits des pavillons, la coupole bleue de l'hôpital, et la maison des gardiens derrière le potager (dans la chambre du fond Jules Galles agonise: il parle encore quelques mots de breton pour maudire sa descendance; patois et noms propres, c'est de lui que j'apprends les langues impures).

Un enfant se penche au balcon où il apprend le vertige, et poussé par l'auteur qui s'est approché dans son dos, il tombe mais sa chute est légère sur les graviers: pas d'épouvante et personne aux fenêtres.

Il se souvient de sa mère qui sûrement le croit mort, et remonte lentement les escaliers pour lui faire peur. Elle, en chemise de nuit, elle est folle et ne peut déjà plus crier.

*

Entre le théâtre et les bois, sur le pré où joue toujours, un peu plus déréglé, le clavecin de Rimbaud, il y a la maison de la mère Fanny. Dans la façade grise, entre deux fenêtres aveugles, la porte est encore entrouverte au-dessus de trois marches effondrées, et personne n'oserait pousser les gravats qui font du rez-de-chaussée un lieu où le temps est *tombé*; on devine une table qui n'a jamais été desservie: les assiettes cassées, les couverts sales, tout est resté en l'état, et du sang a séché depuis la mort de la muette.

Since then, the woodwork and the balconies of the red room have crumbled into dust, and the peeling building has been demolished. It is a field of ruins between the path of the mothers, the meadow with the hunters' hide-out, and the milk shed (as the place for meditation is called, the observatory open to the sky and looking onto the milky way: the bedrooms where sometimes blood turns to milk).

*

Beyond begin the suburbs and their murky towns, visible walls and latent gates. Closed shutters, sleep until midday, and the bordering forest much further on: towards Presles and Saint-Leu, Nerville et Villiers-Adam. From which we came back in a sweat after we got lost – in the fear and hope of getting older very quickly.

Gennevilliers is seven leagues away, not using *postillions* or *beasts of dream burden*: we never went that far. But the Orient is at our feet when at nightfall we look over the roofs of the bungalows, the blue cupola of the hospital, and the keepers' lodge behind the kitchen garden (in the back room Jules Galles is dying: he still speaks a few words of Breton to curse his decendence in; patois and proper names, I learn impure languages from him).

A child is leaning over the balcony learning the meaning of vertigo, shoved by the author come up behind him, falls but lightly on the gravel: no horror and no one at the windows.

He remembers his mother who certainly thinks he's dead, and goes slowly up the stairs again to give her a fright. She, in her night-dress, is mad and already unable to cry out.

*

Between the theatre and the woods, on the meadow where Rimbaud's harpsichord is still playing, a little more unruly still, stands Mother Fanny's house. In the middle of the grey façade, between two blind windows, the door is still hanging half-open above three broken steps, and no one would dare push the rubble around which makes the ground floor a place where time has *fallen*: you can make out a table that has never been cleared: the broken plates, the dirty knives and forks, everything has stayed as it was, and blood has dried since the death of the dumb woman who lived there.

Sa mère était cantatrice, et le chant troublant de cette femme, lorsqu'il atteignait les notes les plus hautes, provoquait une saignée telle dans sa gorge qu'elle ne pouvait recommencer avant plusieurs semaines. Aussi, dès que le chant s'élevait, chacun courait-il se terrer chez soi, pour ne rien entendre des dernieres notes déchirantes, pour ne point subir cette blessure aiguë.

Dans cet arrière-monde résonnent encore des bruits en profondeur: les cris des porcs, des oies, et la voix d'un enfant. C'est un jour entre chien et loup, et toute la bestialité de l'heure est réveillée.

*

Aujourd'hui les lecteurs sont dans les loges, mais le parterre reste vide, et ce désert d'ombre fait d'eux des voyeurs par-delà un lieu interdit: voyeurs d'un théâtre miniature, occupants des marges où ils déambulent librement, pour dominer de loin ce qui ne leur appartient pas.

Les rôles sont préparés, les personnages sont en place (le nain, la cantatrice, les mannequins du souffleur…): demain chez le «donneur de rouge» ils joueront sans parole et sans acte une des plus vieilles *passementeries:* mensonge silence et passe dans le temps mort où les mots changent de sens. La scène est éclairée comme un soir sous les marronniers blancs, mais l'auteur nous tourne le dos, car il n'a plus besoin d'aucun rôle. Dans sa loge, sa perruque est accrochée au-dessus du miroir où le père se rasait.

Il parle au dieu du vent, le vieil épouvantail qu'on coiffait du chapeau de l'aïeule, sous le cerisier. Voyeur mort, il a l'air d'observer pour toujours naines blanches et géantes rouges dans les chambres du ciel (la longue galerie des glaces où s'est perdu mon sosie). Sans lui les répétitions recommencent, pour quel opéra dont on n'entendrait que le chant de la rainette, ou les jurons de l'ange (qui n'est peut-être mis là que pour l'amant de nos mères) quand il venait laver sur le carreau le peu de sang qui précédait l'annonciation?

Les miroirs de maintenant sont encombrés de souvenirs plus vrais que nature. Après les basses besognes de la nuit peut commencer le chant où les mots viennent perler comme un lait sanglant de nourrices sèches. Musicienne et muette accroupie à l'écart, la «mère» du récitant accompagne des voix qui n'appartiennent à personne, mais aux masques des acteurs *manqués:* le sosie, le suicidé…

Her mother was an opera singer, and the disturbing song of this woman as it reached the highest notes set off such a flow of blood in her throat that she could not sing again for several weeks. Moreover as soon as the song began to rise, each and every one ran home in terror to avoid hearing any of the last rending notes and being subjected to that piercing wound.

In this hinterland noises still resonate in depth: the cries of pigs and geese and the voice of a child. The light is murky, neither fish nor fowl, and all the bestiality of the hour is awakened.

*

Today the readers are in the boxes, but the stalls are empty and this desert made of shadow makes voyeurs of them, above and beyond a forbidden place: voyeurs spying in a miniature theatre, inhabitants of margins where they walk freely and dominate from afar what does not belong to them.

The parts are prepared, the characters in place (the dwarf, the singer, the prompter's puppets...) tomorrow at make-up they will act without words or movements one of the oldest of *theatrical trimmings*: lie silence and a forward pass into that dead time in which words change sense. The scene is lit like an evening under white chestnut trees, but the author turns his back on us, for he no longer needs a role. In his dressing room, his wig is hung over the mirror where the father used to shave.

He speaks to the god of the wind, the old scarecrow with the grandmother's hat under the cherry tree. As a dead voyeur he seems to observe white dwarfesses forever and red giantesses in the chambers of the heavens (the long gallery of mirrors in which my double got lost). Without him the rehearsals begin again, for which opera, you hear only the song of the tree-frog, or the oaths of the angel (who perhaps has only been put there for our mother's lovers) when he came to wash from the tiles the spot of blood which preceded the annunciation?

Today's mirrors are cluttered with memories truer than life. After the menial tasks of the night the song can begin in which words come foaming up like bloody milk from wetnurses run dry. A musician squatting mute to one side, she's the 'mother' of the recitalist and accompanies voices belonging to no one but the masks of *failed* actors: understudy, suicide...

Une sœur laide et froide s'est ouvert les veines au fond de la bibliothèque, sous un ciel d'or et de neige. Pendant les quelques heures de son sommeil d'amour, cette insolation du désir à l'ombre des livres, elle a caressé dans son corps un enfant bègue et un jeune homme impuissant, qui ont fini par s'endormir à leur tour. Alors, comme une morsure à son oreille, la vieille fille a entendu, peut-être murmurés par l'un d'eux, les mots qu'elle avait jusque-là retenus sur ses lèvres.

A cold ugly sister has opened her veins in the depths of the library beneath a sky of gold and snow. For the few hours of her sleep of love, that insulation from desire in the shadow of the books, she caressed a stammering child within her body and an impotent young man who in the end both fell asleep. Then, like a bite on the ear, the old maid heard the words, murmured by one of them perhaps, she had until then kept behind her lips.

I

Vers néandertal et son théâtre désert le sommeil continue dos
tourné le rôle funèbre du souffleur (arabe et chacal il chasse les
désirs et casse la faïence nocturne avant de renverser le seau
sanglant de barbe bleue (la vaisselle de nuit de narcisse où les
amoureuses venaient rincer leurs chiffons les mouchoirs d'indicibles
fanfreluches les falbalas de l'ineffable et voilettes des veuves (loin
de ma vue lingeries de rien mes yeux de myope ont trop vu les
promeneuses et la septième de porte en escalier par les conversations
séculaires ouvre déjà la chambre vide de ma mort (il pleut par-
tout quand pandore ouvre ses boîtes et des mantes avant mariage
viennent du dehors pour dévorer mes provisions (des mots
manquent déjà dans le cortège de mes deuils on ne vendra rien de
moi de mes secrets dévalisés tout se retrouvera dans la monnaie
du somnambule (je donne au lecteur à la lente élocution les nom-
brils de nos pères et l'ombilic long du langage mais l'espace ne se
remplira pas trop de hoquets lactés renvoient les paroles et la
semence avec les mots énormes qu'on voyait de trop près derrière
le regard grossissant de nos mères (dans leurs maisons de saveurs
les géants devant la porte poussent des armoires et les têtes réduites
des auteurs (et mon lit clos   mes malles de chiffons   ma
chaise percée   mes buffets défendus   mes pommes
de douleurs   la pierre à mémoire (la baignoire de marat les
charrettes sous la terreur l'histoire déménage son décor sous la peur
du rouge et du tiers état (commode empire et costume d'apparat
dans ses prairies de terreur blanche elle recule sa fin vers le soir et
son théâtre de veuves (centenaires solennelles à prédire les lunaisons
pauvres poules accroupies devant mon sosie qu'on saigne jusqu'au
sens (dans les maisons démesurées j'étais derrière les miroirs où le
père se rasait me laissant saigner noir par les sangsues matinales
(elles avaient ma voix d'opéra les petites pieuvres emmurées dans
les ruines et restes diurnes d'un cauchemar (au réveil de milliers
de morts analogiques des sauterelles emmaillotées bouffent mes
organes de bègue et traînent la dépouille du dormeur à l'entrée du
passage grêle de la mort (un peu de nuit dans l'anus déculotté déjà
je cours derrière les bâtardises du sens avant de tomber dans mon
corps l'opéra de voix off (ma mère cantatrice compte les pages de
mes confessions froides et les vingt et un grammes perdus dans
les vérités vertes du réel (dans un repas rituel le poids des mots
mangés crus par le lecteur et les bruits de sa bouche entre un mort

I

At about neanderthal and its deserted theatre sleep with its back
turned carries on the funereal role of the prompter (as an arab and a
jackal he chases away desires and breaks the nocturnal china before
knocking over bluebeard's bloody pail (the night crockery of narcissus
where women in love would come to wash their glad rags the kerchiefs
of inexpressible fripperies the flounces of the ineffable and widow's
weeds (flimsy lingerie far from my sight my short-sighted eyes have
seen too many streetwalkers and the seventh from door to staircase
through the conversations of the centuries already opens the door to
empty bedroom of my death (it rains everywhere when pandora opens
her boxes and mantises before marriage come in from outside to
devour my provisions (words fail already in the procession of those
I mourn nothing of mine will be sold none of my burgled secrets
everything will turn up again in the small change of the sleepwalker
(I give readers with slow elocution the navels of our fathers and the
long umbilical cord of language but the space will not be filled too
many milky hiccoughs send back the voice and the seed with the
enormous words that we saw from too near behind the impregnating
gaze of our mothers (in their houses made of savour the giants at the
door push the cupboards and the miniaturised heads of the authors
(and my curtained bed   my trunks full of rags   my chair
with a hole in the seat   my forbidden sideboard   my apples
of pain   the memory stone (marat's bathtub the tumbrils during
the terror history moves its decor for fear of the scarlet and the third
estate (empire chest ceremonial costume in its meadows of white
terror postponing its completion until evening and its theatre of
widows (ancient women solemn in predicting lunar months poor
wenches squatting in front of my double being bled right up to the
sense (in the outsize houses I stood behind the mirrors in which my
father shaved leaving me to be bled black by the morning leeches (they
had my operatic voice the poor little octopuses walled up in the ruins
and the diurnal remains of a nightmare (at the awakening of thousands
of analogical deaths swaddled grasshoppers scoff my stammering
organs and drag the sleeper's remains to the meagre door of death
(a little night in the bare-arsed anus already I'm running behind the
bastardisings of meaning before falling into my body an opera of voices
off (my mother the singer counts the pages of my cold confessions
and the twenty-one grammes lost in the scandalous truths of the real
(in a ritual meal the weight of words eaten raw by the reader and

et la mort (loin du bric à brac de baignoires et perroquets devant les promeneurs posthumes les déménageurs porteront mon mannequin (sept ans de malheur pour mon sosie l'assassin exsangue au bas de l'escalier venu tirer la sonnette et la corde du pendu (ma vie bien après moi c'est du bleu dans la chimie des climats la météo bavarde annonçant ma venue prochaine et des vents de poussière (un immeuble soufflé c'est la fin du théâtre…

*

(une explosion lente de paroles sous le voile prêt à s'ouvrir moins originel que la mère gigogne et son ciel de culottes bouffantes (marionnette ancien régime un peuple de nains traîne ses sacs sur nos tréteaux de parodie (des loges de grévin ses fils astrologues ou chirurgiens la regardent en répétant leurs monologues (lazare et marat   abraham et landru   hamlet et ménélas   et la fille de minos pour un romancier séducteur a délacé l'a noir de son corset (l'acteur emporte le cothurne ce soulier haut de vénus où je cachais mes sœurs samothraces et mes amoureuses mutilées (elles se déshabillent aujourd'hui dans l'atelier de couture mon frère défenestré regarde la scène et du haut du tilleul il voit encore mes comédiennes (le froid qui s'en va de leurs bouches annonce la nuit sur les théâtres à l'italienne où tout se terminera par une voix blanche et le miroir d'un miroir (souffleur souffre douleur ta tête est provisoire déjà réduite à la taille troglodyte au fond des chambres de pierre où pose pour un pére teinturier la vénus rouge de milo (scène après scène c'est la même suite de sésames et le vol violoncelle des chauves souris les vampires venus boire le sang pâle de l'inceste (poète puritain dans le linceul triple de lazare ne te retourne pas sur tes sœurs et sors du caveau familial où rien n'arrivera plus ex machina (dieu dans le trou du souffleur a perdu sa voix de castrat l'aphasie des femmes pourrait le consoler mais sur leurs lèvres il lit le récit de sa fin l'opéra parlé dont un clavecin silencieux joue déjà l'ouverture (on m'endort sous le masque et mon corps ouvert à son tour c'est dedans qu'il faudrait voir un théâtre minuscule (l'ombre du nain   l'apparition de l'acteur   la voix du sang   la scène du sacrifice   l'aïeul énorme et ma mère cardinale   mon carré d'oncles et de reines   mes sœurs

the noises of his mouth between someone and death (somewhere far
from the bric-à-brac of bathtubs and hat stands in front of the post-
humous strollers the removal men will carry off my mannequin (seven
years' bad luck for my double the deathly pale assassin at the bottom
of the stairs come to pull the bell and the hanged man's rope (my life
long after me is that blue in the chemistry of the climates the chatter-
box weather forecast predicting my near future and winds of dust (a
building whispered by the prompter this is the end of the theatre...

*

(a slow explosion of words under the veil ready to open but less
original than the old woman who lived in a shoe and her horizon of
baggy pants (an *ancien régime* puppet a people of dwarfs drags its
bags onto our parody boards (from box seats at madame tussaud's
her astrologer or surgeon sons watch her as they learn their mono-
logues (lazarus and marat   abraham and landru   hamlet
and menelaus   and for a seductive novelist the daughter of
minos has unlaced the black a of her corset (the actor carries off the
buskin that high-soled venus slipper in which I would hide my
samothracian sisters and my mutilated lovers (today they undress
in the seamstress's shop my defenestrated brother watches the scene
and from the top of the lime tree he can still see my actresses (the
cold coming from their mouths ushers in the night over the italian
style theatres where everything will come to an end with a white
voice and the mirror of a mirror (prompter scapegoat your head is
provisional reduced already to troglodyte size in the depths of the
stone rooms where the red venus de milo poses for a father-dyer
(scene after scene the same sequence of sesames and the cello-toned
flight of the bats the vampires come to drink the pale blood of incest
(puritan poet in the triple shroud of lazarus do not turn back to
your sisters leave the family cave where nothing ex machina will
happen anymore (in the prompter's box god has lost his castrato
voice the women's aphasia might console him but on their lips he
reads the story of his end spoken opera already a silent harpsi-
chord is playing the overture (they put me to sleep under the mask
and my body open in turn there inside is where you should get sight
of a tiny theatre (the shadow of the dwarf   the appearance of
the actor   the voice of blood   the scene of sacrifice   the

somnambules   et le mauvais rôle d'orphée (de chant final en rechutes après trois jours de relâche on continue à parler sur d'impossibles proses interrompues...

*

(entre naines blanches et géantes rouges dans les chambres du ciel on a rangé les vêtements de nuit de narcisse dont la doublure descend nue dans le trou du souffleur (l'ombre d'un homme à la tournure de reine la moitié de son corps est morte en miroir l'autre en maison rousse continue de marmonner des romans (au fond d'une loge louée par la mort un singe souffle le sens dans mon corps sans organe et son anatomie imaginée (la bouche des naissances et l'anus des nuits   l'oreille interne et trois osselets   la saignée blanche et les rêves de grossesse   la main noire et les phalanges futures (le lecteur à venir est déjà dans vos yeux lisant par dessus l'épaule de l'homme gauche qui vous tourne le dos pour parler au dieu du vent (centenaire et frappé par la foudre son rire noir secoue l'arbre du dehors et tombent les promesses de salut les litanies les romans perpétuels (l'auteur pour s'entendre parler vient encore dans ma bouche mais là se levant de la chaise dernière sa doublure renverse les rôles et met sa voix par dessus tout...

enormous grandfather and my cardinal mother   my full house of
uncles and queens   my sleepwalking sisters   and orpheus the
bad part (from final aria to relapses after three days' closure we go
on talking about impossible interrupted pieces of prose...

*

(between white dwarfesses and red giantesses in the bedrooms of
the heavens the nightclothes of narcissus have been put away his
understudy comes down naked into the prompter's hole (the shadow
of a man with the figure of a queen half his body is dead in the
mirror the other in the russet house carries on mumbling novels
(standing at the back of a box taken by death a monkey prompter
breathes sense into my organless body and its imagined anatomy
(the mouth of births and the anus of the nights   the inner ear
and three knucklebones   fruitless blood-letting and dreams of
pregnancy   the black hand and the phalanxes of the future (in
your eyes the reader to come is already reading over the shoulder
of that cackhanded man turning his back to talk to the god of the
wind (ancient and struck by lightning his black laughter shakes
the tree from the outside and down come promises of salvation
the litanies the never-ending tales (the author just to hear himself
speak still comes into my mouth but now getting up from the
chair behind his understudy he reverses the roles and projects his
voice over everything...

II

L'ouvrier ivre mort au métier d'un seul livre en chinant les langages augmente la lecture d'un orient dérisoire comme reine des belges ou maid of china les échantillons potagers d'un peuple sans mémoire (l'écriture morphine après morphine et les mots longs en bouche à remplacer le dégoût de tabac le temps pourrait finir dans les fumeries de mars (les laitues lactées d'oubli les os de lapins nettoyés par l'histoire naturelle et les têtes au fond de l'abdomen histoire de nos famines la terre se souvient du crétacé sous les odeurs de cidre et de javel (le corps criblé de sable et d'un grand bleu le réel monsieur c'est ce cresson de nuages au dessus de l'afrique affamée (l'aïeule rêve de la chambre bleu ciel où se voir comme caillou sur la table de nuit le souvenir de soi même après passage des peigneuses et litanies des médisants (angine et mélancolie   scarlatine et tremblements   migraine et tétanie angoisse et varicelle   (longtemps muet dans ma langue au milieu de mes sœurs somnambules je vivais des nuits césariennes entre querelle et jardin (un vrai planétarium où le père illettré nous délivrait du sens et de l'inceste nos phrases incisées cette pluie rouge entre désert et sahara (l'ébéniste noir ouvrait ses charades et rabotait la verrue molle de l'histoire où clapote encore une marée de petites morts (dans mes plages intimes j'ai enterré cent fois le père mausolée que mes phrases défont maison précaire où j'enfouis ce qui tombe (l'ombilic et l'ongle de l'orteil   paroles et dents de lait   l'or apatride des métaphores   ma tête italique et tous mes totems (derrière le divan je recommence le roman l'envie pure de prononcer mes surnoms mes règnes et mes tabous par la bouche utérine (ma sœur liseuse d'aigle et sa voix d'orthophoniste à prononcer les morts qu'on change au panthéon le coffre aux tiroirs écrits dans le jardin de geneviève ils goûteraient bien l'aphasie pour le plaisir de répéter crénom en cassant la machine bègue où bute le symbole (sirène sereine   rima mari   bribes de scribe ragots d'argot   nulle lune   affirme frimas   et singe signe maigre magie

*

II

The workman blind drunk at the loom of a single book dyes the
languages and increases the readership of a derisory orient like queen
of the belgians or the maid of china the cottage-garden samples of a
people without memory (writing shot after shot of morphine and
words staying long in the mouth replace the foul taste of tobacco
time might end in the smoking dens of march (the milky lettuces of
oblivion rabbit bones picked clean by natural history and their heads in
the depths of the abdomen history of our famines the earth remembers
the cretaceous age beneath the smells of cider and disinfectant (body
riddled with sand and a large bruise the real gaffer is that watercress
cloud above starving africa (the grandmother dreams of the sky-blue
bedroom and of seeing herself there as a pebble on the bedside table
the memory of self even after the dressers and the scandalmongers'
litanies have gone (angina and melancholy   scarlet fever and the
shakes   migraine and tetanus   anxiety and chickenpox   (long
since dumb in my tongue among my sleepwalking sisters I lived
cesarian nights between disputes and horticulture (a real planetarium
where the illiterate father freed us from sense and incest our incised
sentences that red rain between desert and sahara (the black cabinet
maker would open charades and plane the soft wart of history in
which there still laps a tide of orgasm (a hundred times I have buried
the father in my intimate beaches a mausoleum that my sentences
undo a precarious home where I stuff everything that falls (umbilical
cord and toe-nail   words and milk teeth   the stateless gold of
metaphors   the italics part of my brain and all my totems (behind
the sofa I begin the novel again the pure desire to utter my surnames
my reigns and my taboos from a uterine mouth (my sister eagle-eyed
reader her speech therapist's voice sounding the dead changed in
the pantheon that chest with drawers written in guenevere's garden
they would happily sample aphasia for the pleasure of repeating damn
and blast and breaking the stammering machine where the symbol
stumbles (siren serene   groom room   scraps of scribe   malice
alice   moon at noon   affirm infirm   and mime sign   meagre
magic

*

(habits d'averses et de reprises l'aïeule est encore là marchande à la toilette qui raccommode sous le cerisier puis compte les pas d'un désert froid de cinq mille ans mais personne ne viendra plus du côté de montmorency car la maison des petites coutumes va changer de propriétaire l'espion le loup le vigilant déménagent de nuit le mobilier du jargonneur (le fond du déluge est trop froid noé délivre-moi de tes fils mouillant mon lit ces batraciens debout qui fument après l'amour cigare du soir et mégot du matin leur mère à mon insu leur apprendra l'inceste et la toilette de ma mort (retournée dans ma bouche la mort mâche mes régions natales repas de la mémoire au fond des larmes un monstre radote sans souvenir du grossissement trois fois de ma tête (veau aveugle il lèche mes plaies les pertes blanches et petites morts et sous mes mots écorchés la vérité lâche ses chiens (du balcon de babel c'est la curée sur ma mère cardinale et côté jargon ce nain des antipodes mais c'est mon père rabougri de son doigt mutilé me montrant le bourreau dans les linges rougis (mais non c'est l'orient qui tord ses chiffons la bure le linceul et la moitié sinistre du livre au firmament refermé de nos morts qui laissent parler l'intitulé (les aléas de l'alphabet   les vestibules de barbe bleue   placards de l'adultère   la maison de matelas   armoire à galaxies pharmacie d'un dieu contagieux   son héritage de rougeoles et reliquaires   et le ciel dessus dessous (de chambre en chambre et de nuits blanches en portes bleues le piéton des songes peut bien chercher la chaise où les âges s'assoient les quatre pères cardinaux déménagent le mobilier (mon père sous son matelas mouille les linges que ma mère lave à l'étage les loques trempées de sueur et bientôt les dentelles au balcon (intermèdes humides où naissent mes romans minuscules ces boîtiers de pacotille où je serre mes secrets lourds l'œillet mouillé de sang le bouton de fraise à cueillir et l'abricot velu tombé là (vers un jardin moins japonais que nulle part ou vers le lit profond du chaos nos métaphores manivelles minuscules ne renversent jamais l'œil et ses milliards de points aveugles (mouches à reculons loin de l'eternel sous la poche de ses eaux après le déluge après babel hors des maisons démeublées les amoureuses énormes roulent un rocher végétal (l'entrée par l'hymen la sortie par le tympan quelle quarantaine dans nos corps et la terre par dessus…

(outfits for showers and full of patches the grandmother is still there dealing in wardrobes mending under the cherry tree then counts the steps in a desert with the cold of five thousand years but no one will come again along montmorency way for the house of little habits is about to change hands the spy the wolf the watchman move the jargon monger's furniture out by night (the depths of the flood are too cold noah free me of your sons wetting my bed those batrachians stand smoking a cigar after making love in the evening and a fag-end in the morning their mother will teach them incest without my knowing and how to dress my corpse (turning round in my mouth death masticates the regions of my birth a meal of memory in the depth of tears a monster rambles without remembering the triple swelling of my head (a blind calf he licks my wounds the white discharges and orgasms and beneath my flayed words truth lets loose its dogs (from babel's balcony there is a mad rush on my cardinal mother and from over by the jargon that antipodean dwarf oh it's my stunted father pointing his mutilated finger at the executioner in the blood-stained linen (no it's the orient wringing out its rags the frock the shroud and the dark half of the book with the enclosed firmament of our dead who let the title speak (the hazards of the alphabet   bluebeard's vestibules   wardrobes of adultery
the house of mattresses   the galaxy cupboard   the pharmacy of a contagious god   his legacy of measles and reliquaries   and the sky turned upside down (from room to room and from white sleepless nights to blue doors the walker of your dreams can search all he likes for the chair where the ages sit the four cardinal fathers are moving the furniture out (beneath his mattress my father wets the linen that my mother washes upstairs rags and tatters soaked in sweat and soon the lace on the balcony (moist moments where my miniature novels are born those tin-pot watch-cases where I clasp my heavy secrets the carnation moist with blood the strawberry bud ripe and ready to be plucked and the downy apricot fallen right there (towards a garden less japanese than anywhere or towards the deep bed of chaos our metaphors those miniature cranks never upend their eyes and the millions of blind spots there (specks flying backwards far from the eternal under the pocket of its waters after the flood after babel out of the empty houses the enormous women in love roll a vegetal rock (entry via the hymen exit via the tympanum what forty days and nights in the body and the earth on top...

III

Âne noir en deuil d'un soleil double à qui les mots manquaient
devant la flore à nommer il te reste à braire le langage et rire de
tes métamorphoses en couvant la carcasse d'icare (une mâchoire
entre miroir et maison bleue sur le pré où joue toujours un peu
plus déréglé le clavecin de rimbaud car le temps se déboîte et le
corps désossé du songe (l'âne et le singe avant les gelées blanches
échangent leurs messes basses en riant de la bêtise du sphinx (plus
d'ailes ni de paroles mais le paletot troué de l'aïeule pour ce vieil
épouvantail qu'on brûle à l'entrée de l'hiver (sous le regard de
l'idiot traînant après soi le remords d'être mâle quand le vent dans
ses pâleurs ramène des histoires révolues comme entre chien et
loup la venue d'un aveugle (la chambre double de son œil est un
bordel pour demi dieux la rivière sans lit de leurs souvenirs leur
sert ici de miroir (une haie d'hortensias des édredons d'oiseaux
rouges voici l'hôtel où le temps passe en cardinal ordinaire (sous
sa nudité bleu nuit je vois une marque de naissance la main de son
père vidant un lapin de son sang (une famille se déchire et laisse
un orphelin défroqué seul sur une prairie de silences à chercher
l'entrée de son corps (l'oreille ou les trous de mémoire   l'anus ou
la pupille ou la bouche béante et sans parole   vieille lune inondée
sous les périodes du ciel (les animaux du déluge au sahara d'avant
désert ânonnent l'histoire et vont boire vers le nord où le lièvre a
oublié son nom (et son prénom dans un pays de prose de raisins
noirs et de mûres tous les fruits tombés rouges dans la géographie
de mes phrases (l'idiot sous les feuillages regarde encore le vol des
augures et pleure en écorchant son propre nom d'oiseau (rossignol
bègue mourant dans la main chaude et rêvant sous les tabliers
noirs de bretagne un ailleurs de lait caillé de marronniers nains de
mascarets (de mongolie sous les coiffes tourterelles et leur ventre
tremblant quand la terre montre ses graines à des filles mères de
l'orient (lavées de leurs péchés par les chiens de l'orage qui boivent
le sang sur le velours et l'urine des chats (blancs comme le linge
tellement rincé de nos morts les petits fils à l'âge de raison s'en
vont vers un champ de pavots pour traverser le sommeil et la mer
rouge...

*

III

Black ass in mourning for a double sun for whom words fail faced with the flora to be named you have but to bray language and laugh at your metamorphoses as you hatch the carcass of icarus (a jawbone between mirror and blue house on the meadow where rimbaud's harpsichord plays ever more out of synch for time is out of joint and the boned body of dream (the ass and the monkey exchange their low masses before the white frosts and laugh at the sphinx's stupidity (no more wings nor words but the grandmother's cardigan with holes in it given to that old scarecrow burnt at the coming of winter (under the idiot's gaze as he drags the shame of being male behind him when the wind in its pallors brings back stories of time past like the arrival of a blind man in the twilight (the double chamber of his eye is a brothel for demi gods the bedless river of their memories acts here as their mirror (a hortensia hedge eiderdowns of red birds here is the hotel where time passes through the cardinal hours (beneath its midnight blue nakedness I see a birthmark the hand of his father draining a rabbit of its blood (a family tears itself apart and leaves a defrocked orphan alone on a meadow of silences looking for the entry to his body (the ear or the holes in memory   the anus or the pupil or the gaping wordless mouth   old moon swamped beneath the periods of the sky (the animals of the flood in the sahara before it was desert stumble their braying way through the story and go and drink to the north where the hare forgot its name (and its forename in a land of prose of black grapes and blackberries all the fruit fallen red into the geography of my sentences (the idiot beneath the branches still watches the flight of the omens and weeps as he flays his own bird's name (stammering nightingale dying in a warm hand and dreaming under the black aprons of brittany an elsewhere of clotted milk and dwarf chestnut trees and tidal waves (from mongolia under the turtledove head-dresses and their belly trembling when the earth shows its grain to the unmarried mothers of the orient (washed of their sins by the dogs of the storm who drink the blood on velvet and cats' urine (white as the oh so rinsed linen of our dead our grandsons at the age of reason go off to a field of poppies to cross sleep and the red sea...

*

(le lavoir où l'enfant naturel vient prononcer son nom de famille avant la mue complète de sa voix (basse et blanche car il finira phoque en enfer musical ou maître fou dans les chambres de l'ouïe quand il faut frapper comme un sourd (avant la parole après l'oubli derrière l'hymen on entendait tout de vos paradis intestins (vos bruits d'entrailles   de vielle et de viole   vos propos roturiers vos souvenirs véniels   et votre argot d'amour (argonautes à la toison grisonnante on n'entend plus sur l'oreiller vos romans d'avant hier et derrière la cloison vos colères d'alcôve (ni dans vos lits clos les sœurs de lait qu'on saignait mais minuit passe au rouge avec trois jours de retard (des parents proches dont la parole vire au noir deviennent les patients personnages qu'on vouvoie dans le sommeil (à la noël on leur porte à manger car ils commencent à trouver bon le pain sous la neige et mûres les groseilles des morts (l'âne va bientôt brouter la ciguë ses descendants ne sauront rien de l'abreuvoir et des loups (le nu dans le miroir n'aura plus peur des nuits blanches ni des habits de deuil qu'on se passait de mère en fille la dernière s'est mise à rire devant son père travesti (un homme apparu pour mardi gras dans la région des demoiselles où les générations se suivent et s'assoient sur la pierre frottée (jules et rose galles   hermine et moïse bloch   léonie veuve et enterrée   léon marie l'enfant reconnu   irène simone aux yeux verts (leurs noms ne parlent encore à personne mais nos parents à sang froid sont des morts en train de muer…

*

(quelques mots d'anatomie quelques noms de famille un fauteuil en osier devant la porte où la mort avant merle a parlé son patois (rôle et comparaison trois floraisons noires et la comédie d'après crapaud le vocabulaire hurlant à la lune (bois chique bois chandelle   bois citron bois cochon   bois corail bois flambeau   bois la glu bois guillaume   bois marie bois rivière   bois rouge et vents de fraise   vents de chêne et veaux de mars   mais le vrai vent c'est la risée dans un public de grands ducs et d'effraies (d'un théâtre de sourds en dormant j'entends les rires et sans raison chez les morts la monnaie de la passe (les mots dans la

(the wash-house where the natural child comes to utter his family
name before the complete breaking of his voice (low and blank for
he will finish up huffing and puffing in a musical hell or master
madman in the chambers of hearing when it's time to beat like the
deaf (before speech after oblivion behind the hymen all of your
intestinal paradise was to be heard (the noises of your entrails
hurdy-gurdy and viola   your belch remarks   your venial
memories   and your argot of love (argonauts with greying
fleece your yesterday novels are no longer heard on the pillow and
your alcove anger behind the screen (nor the foster sisters being
bled in your box beds but midnight passes to red three days late
(close relatives whose words veer to the black become the patient
figures politely addressed in dream (at christmas food is taken to
them for they acquire a taste for bread under the snow and ripe
the redcurrants of the dead (the ass is soon grazing on hemlock its
descendants will know nothing of the trough and the wolves (the
nude in the mirror will fear sleepless nights no more nor the
mourning clothes passed from mother to daughter she started to
laugh at her transvestite father (a man appeared for mardi gras in
the young women's patch where the generations follow and sit on the
worn stone (jules and rose galles   hermine and moses bloch
léonie widowed and buried   léon marie the legitimate child
irène simone with the green eyes (their names don't yet speak to any-
one but our cold-blooded parents are dead and shedding their skin…

*

(a few words of anatomy a few family names a wicker chair in front
of the door where death before magpies spoke in its dialect (a role
and a comparison three dark flowerings and the play in toad-speak
a vocabulary yelling at the moon (chewing wood and tallow wood
lemon-tree wood and lewd-tree wood   coral wood and torch
wood   leech wood and kaiser wood   drink mary drink river
redwood and strawberry winds   oak winds and march mammon
but the real wind is the mockery in a crowd of dukes and barn
owls (from a theatre of the deaf as I slept I heard the laughter and
for no reason change from a trick amongst the dead (words at home

maison n'ont plus que des bruits d'os un an déjà qu'on emportait mon langage avec l'accent de la chouette et celui du charlatan (le mobilier des morts est dans la cour avec le sommier noir où l'enfant défenestré finira bien par tomber et se taire (entre la barque et les bois de lit quels massacres d'amoureuses et de tortues endormies sous les penderies d'ébène (une nuit sans sommeil et derrière les jalousies le miroir est aveugle où les mariés se regardaient mourir (larmes de cire et perruques rousses les voilà dépouillés de leurs parures sous les masques du deuil (côté cour ils suivent du regard l'enfant bagué le messager maintenant sans parole qui passait des heures à cueillir le bouton de chair et l'œillet (le chasse diable à mille trous   l'œil de dieu compagnon blanc   la mort aux oies et à socrate   l'herbe à thérèse et la véronique femelle (sur les prairies hermaphrodites il mettra demain leur linge à blanchir et retournera les lits (il enfile aujourd'hui leurs chemises pour réciter leurs rôles en changeant la donne des noms...

only make the noise of bones a year ago already my luggage was taken away with its charlatan's accent and the owl's (the furniture of the dead is in the courtyard and along with the black boxsprings that the defenestrated child will soon end up falling into that way he'll be quiet (between the boat and the wooden beds what a massacre of lovers and tortoises sleeping under the ebony wardrobes (a sleepless night and behind the screens the mirror has gone blind in which the newly-weds would watch each other die (wax tears and red wigs now the newly-weds are bereft of all that finery under their mourning masks (in the courtyard they watch the child with rings on his fingers the messenger now without words would spend hours picking flesh-buds and carnations (the threadbare scare-devil

the eye of god the white companion   death to the geese and and to socrates   theresa weed and the female veronica (tomorrow he'll put their washing out to be cleaned in the hermaphrodite prairies and turn the beds (today he puts on their shirts recites their parts and shuffles the names...

IV

De la loge où nichaient les cigognes trois musiciens tête bêche ont
entendu les cris de l'accouchée (une portée de rats sur le navire
perdant ses eaux s'enfuit en suivant le violon de la fosse et voilà
ma mère dans l'opéra des douleurs (son chant d'écorchée les soirs
d'anniversaire monte encore à l'entresol avec les râles du petit
mort l'enfant trouvé d'une sirène et d'un père naturel (le mort a
changé sous les masques de l'autre et c'est carnaval dans les chambres
où l'on chassait de mémoire d'homme (à la belle étoile on boit le
lait des aïeules en attendant le dernier convive un vieillard bien
après moi qui grandit sur mes genoux (entre trompe et tambour je
lui parle dans l'oreille et l'endors pour l'hiver en comptant les jours
où je coucherai dans son corps (un monument d'os où dorment
les mendiants leurs songes dans le panier sont des rois de chiffons
les époux sanglants des blanchisseuses (sous les paupières des
dormeurs elles battent le linge toute la nuit j'entends les ouvrières
laver le rouge et les mouchoirs (écrevisses en vierge elles remontent
les eaux pour aller mourir dans le ventre vide des pères…

*

(en imitant le chant des mâles un orphelin sous son domino noir
danse la parade et l'agonie (une voix de corbeau mais trop tard pour
les augures c'est la veuve du menuisier qu'on annonce dans les bois
(chêne ou contrebasse un sanglier vient derrière elle et renifle la
mort dans nos noces contre nature (un buffet plein d'ail et l'armoire
au carrefour c'est le débarras des vivants leurs déguisements dehors
pour un théâtre à la criée (chiffons peaux de lapins quels rôles
ambulants pour quelques centimes et la monnaie qui tombe avec
la nuit (l'ourse et le chariot voici l'exode sous les noms du ciel et
la constellation de l'animal qui met bas (qui vêle sous sa chevelure
et se relève pour voir un troupeau de géantes à l'entrée du souffleur
(aïeules en quarantaine elles mangent nos mots mais les rats s'en
vont de leurs bouches en poussant des cris d'amour on les entend
sous terre ameuter leurs petits pour qu'ils imitent nos phrases (dans
leur descendance il manque un vendredi la case oubliée de babel
ce château nul où l'hier passe toujours avant l'aujourd'hui (quand

IV

From the box in which the storks were nesting three musicians
top to tail heard the cries of the woman in labour (a litter of rats
flees from the ship losing its waters and follows the graveyard
violin there is my mother in the opera of pain (her flayed body
song on birthday evenings still rises to the mezzanine with the
death rattles of the young child foundling of a siren and a natural
father (the dead child changed under the masks of the other and
carnival reigns in the rooms where people have hunted throughout
living memory (under the stars we drink the grandmothers' milk
waiting for the last guest an old man well after my time growing
on my knee (between trumpet and drum I speak in his ear and
put him to sleep for the winter counting the days until I shall
sleep in his body (a monument of bones where beggars sleep their
dreams in the basket are rag kings the bloody husbands of the
washerwomen (under the sleepers' eyelids they beat the linen all
night long I hear the women working washing the rouge and the
kerchiefs (virginal crayfish they struggle upstream to go and die in
the empty bellies of the fathers...

*

(imitating the song of the males an orphan in his black domino
dances a parade and the death throes (a crow's voice but too late
for the omens it's the carpenter's widow announced in the woods
(oak or double-bass a wild boar comes in her wake and sniffs death
in our unnatural wedding feasts (a sideboard full of garlic and the
cupboard at the crossroads it's all the junkroom of the living their
disguises put out for a theatre auction (rags rabbit skins what roving
roles for a few coppers and the change dropping with the night (the
bear and the plough here's the exodus under the names of the
heavens and the constellation of the animal about to drop (calving
under its hair and rises to see a herd of giants at the prompter's
entrance (grandmothers in quarantine they eat our words but the
rats flee their mouths squealing cries of love you can hear them
underground stirring up their young to imitate our sentences (in
their lineage there is a friday missing the missed out space of babel
that nothing castle where yesterday always comes before today (when

le temps double la mise on me trouve à dormir dans la galerie des glaces où s'est perdu mon sosie (pour le revoir paupières closes une main d'amoureuse va bientôt soulever le drap qu'on enlève au rêveur avec la nappe et les viandes (on le présente aux marchands qui le porteront à dos d'homme vers les linges et l'avalanche à l'orifice du rouge féminin...

*

(l'oisellerie s'éloigne à la muette et le nom des choses est sous la bâche des morts qui descendent après moi la scala de l'enfer (nuit et jour ils me parlent au miroir le sommeil est dans leur voix de vautour quand il se pose à l'avant de la barque (au lavoir où le lait tourne en sang les filles à marier viennent se laver des amants de leurs mères (mémoire mort née mon père en moi remue encore je lui donne avec mon nom les offrandes au langage (les blasphèmes et les sifflantes   les vélaires et les labiales   et nos viscères dans les vases   après la chair et le sommeil

time doubles its money you will find me sleeping in the gallery of
mirrors where my double got lost (to see him again eyelids closed
a loving woman's hand will soon lift the sheet snatched from the
dreamer with the tablecloth and the meats (he is presented to the
merchants who will carry him on their backs towards the linen
and the avalanche with the orifice of feminine red...

*

(the bird-house moves stealthily away and the name of things lies
beneath the coarse canvas of the dead coming down behind me the
scala of hell (night and day they speak to me in the mirror sleep
lies in their vulture's voice as it perches on the prow of the boat
(in the wash-house where milk turns to blood the marriageable girls
come to wash clean of their mothers' lovers (still-born memory my
father still moves within me with my name I give him my offerings
to language (the blasphemies and hissers   the velars and the
labials   and our viscera in the vases   after flesh and sleep

V

Derrière la maison des miroirs le récit recommence que murmure
un homme roux pour toujours sur son trône nocturne (un person-
nage sans retenue parle maintenant sous lui lâchant l'or de sa chaise
vers le trou d'une tombe future (dans le derrière du diable une
coquette se contemple et religieuse rose une truie qui réclame des
caresses en riant de mes mots me tend son encrier (le passage d'enfer
est gardé par le chien de nos entrailles qui sait par cœur les modernes
poésies ces cimetières de désirs et de noms propres où dort un
nourrisson rassasié rêvant dans sa bouche la pesée de son corps
sur la balance d'anubis (qui tient la main à plume c'est amenuit
dans la chambre du bavard où toutes les citations se retrouvent à
l'heure de fermeture astres et cicatrices ou titres et citations les
pains perdus d'une faim pharaonique (d'une bouche l'autre un
livre à traverser vivant de tamise en éthiopie la rivière sans lit
saturée de songes biographiques (récits de voyage   fable à tiroirs
       roman moignon   histoire sans histoire   chariot crustacé
       écriture sorcière   anacoluthe à l'origine   bible refoulée
       récit navajo   litote et tabou   parenthèse précaire
passe temps de pénélope   métaphore bafouée   millefeuille et
miettes   archives recopiées   main italique   malherbe ruminée
       orient des grammaires   parlerie de bastille   cancer du
sens   idiome de la mort   étrangère orthographe   étron
nocturne   palace de déraison   ourse de prose   liste de
lettrines   conversations écoutées   roturière mythologie
hérédité sans loi   roman de famille   mausolée de petites morts
       phalanstère d'araignées   machine oubli/retour   titres et
citations   opéra parlé   et collection d'etc. (lecteur à saute
mouton les troupeaux s'en vont de tes paupières pour quel berger
te prenais tu dans les prairies du sommeil (le pissenlit distribue les
feuilles alternées de sa doctrine et jour de la lune/jour de saturne
il souffle au levant les réponses à moitié d'un autre règne (à dos
d'abeille vers un champ d'ignorance la songerie pêle mêle impatiente
n'y touchez pas c'est le pollen précoce de mes nominations…

*

V

Behind the house of mirrors the story starts again murmured by
a redhead forever on his nocturnal throne (a character without
restraint speaks now beneath him dropping the gold from his chair
down towards the hole of a future tomb (a coquette looks at her
image in the backside of the devil and a pink nun a sow demanding
caresses makes fun of my words and hands me her inkwell (the
passage to hell is guarded by the dog of our entrails who knows
the poems of the modern by heart those cemeteries of desires and
proper names where a satiated new-born child sleeps and dreams
the weight of its body in its mouth on the scales of anubis (feather
in hand but it's amenuit in old chatterbox's room where all quot-
ations meet up at closing time stars and scars or titles and quotations
the lost loaves of a pharaonic hunger (from a mouth to another a
book to be crossed living off thames in ethiopia the bedless river
saturated with biographical dreams (travel tales   fable full of
drawers   novel with withered stump   history with no story
      crustacean cart   witchcraft writing   anacoluthia from
the start   repressed bible   navajo tale   litotes and taboo
      precarious parenthesis   penelope's pastime   scorned met-
aphor   cream slice and crumbs   copied out archives
italic handwriting   malherbe remasticated   eastern gramma-
tical promise   talkshop at the bastille   the cancer of sense
      idiom of death   alien spelling   nocturnal turd   palace
of unreason   the great bear in prose   list of latrines   con-
versations overheard   commoner mythology   lawless heredity
      family novel   a mausoleum of orgasms   phalanstery of
spiders   the oblivion/return machine   titles and quotations
      spoken opera   and a collection of etceteras (leap-frogging
reader flocks of sheep go out from your eyes what sort of shepherd
did you take yourself for in the meadows of sleep (the dandelion
gives out alternate sheets of its doctrine and moon-day/saturn-day
whispers to the levant the half-answers of another reign (an impatient
dream hotchpotch on beeback towards a field of ignorance don't
touch it's the precocious pollen of my namings...

*

Sommeil levant je me réveille dans un corps que j'avais cru mouiller avant de m'endormir. On ouvre la boutique de l'embaumeur (où la chouette a vu chavirer le jour), mais c'est une odeur de latrines qui monte des «écuries égyptiennes».

Je sors pour remuer la terre (mes grands-mères mortes se coiffaient sans miroir: instruments aratoires et peignes à démêler, c'est tout ce qu'on trouvera dans leur tombe), et par la porte entrouverte, avec les prophéties du corbeau pénètre «l'âme du bruit» (je m'entends répéter ces trois mots, de la même voix qui récitait les nombres: était-ce le douzième chant de l'odyssée, ou l'énoncé lent des chiffres au loto des pauvres, quand ils jouaient attablés autour des charrettes, sans un regard pour les passants étrangers à leur récréation d'asile?)

Dehors, sous la tonnelle, la servante que je n'ai pas connue tient la tête de mon père entre ses mains (mais j'ai déjà lu cette phrase quelque part, avec la même parenthèse pour évoquer le même faux souvenir).

Une vieille au chignon bas ouvre un livre devant elle, que je tâche de déchiffrer à l'envers. Quand je la reconnais, je me demande où et quand elle a bien pu apprendre à lire. Alors les chairs de son visage se décomposent, et je sens se poser sur moi son œil froid de gallinacée.

«C'est la lèpre des miroirs», dit quelqu'un dans mon dos, prononçant d'une voix blanche les derniers mots d'une langue *déjà* morte.

Eastern sleep I awake in a body I thought I had wet before falling asleep. The embalmer's shop is opening (where the barn owl saw day-light capsize), but there is a smell of latrines rising from the "egyptian stables".

I go out and turn over the earth (my dead grandmothers would do their hair without a mirror: ploughing implements and combs to disentangle with, that's all there will be in their tombs), and through the half-open door along with the crow's prophecies 'the soul of sound' comes in (I can hear myself repeating these four words in the same voice I learnt my numbers in: was it the twelfth canto of the odyssey, or the poor slowly mouthing lottery numbers as they sat around the tumbrils and played, without regard for the foreign passers-by in their asylum-seekers' playtime?)

Outside, under the arbour, the servant whom I never knew is holding my father's head in her hands (I've read that sentence somewhere before, with the same parenthesis evoking the same untrue memory).

An old woman with a drooping chignon opens a book and holds it in front of her, I'm trying to read it back to front. When I recognise her, I wonder where and when she might possibly have learnt to read. And then the fleshes on her face begin to decompose, and I feel her cold galinaceous look turning onto me.

'It's the leper from the mirrors,' somebody says behind me blankly speaking the last words of a language that is *already* dead.

C'est ainsi que la poésie tomba dans la prose, et mon château théâtral dans le troisième *dessous.*

GÉRARD DE NERVAL

Thus poetry fell into prose, and my theatrical castle into the third below.

GÉRARD DE NERVAL

Bois dormant

Wood Asleep

(1983)

Pour mes parents,
ces souvenirs à leur insu

For my parents,
these memories unknown to them

On tourne la page, et derrière une lettre géante (est-ce l'initiale ornée d'un récit en prose régulière, l'arbre fleuri qui cache la forêt d'un blason illisible, où se déchiffre encore, sous les remords et les hésitations du copiste, un signe recopié de travers: une faute d'orthographe ancienne, une erreur d'état civil, bref tout ce qui vient rappeler le mensonge des souvenirs, la honte d'un enfant et la mémoire des noms qu'on craint de perdre malgré tout?) on aperçoit les prairies du sommeil où l'auteur endormi s'est mis à traduire en songe, avant d'être éveillé par l'écho de prophéties à faire peur. En somnambule il reprend alors son voyage du soir, à travers les monuments de la passion mêlant l'universel et l'involontaire: palais idéal, jardin sec, maison de verre, chinoiseries ou villas rococo, posées là au milieu des choux, de la rocaille et des rivières en miroir – tout un désordre apparent où traînent les outils oubliés de la prose.

Plus loin c'est l'étendue des tapis maraîchers, interrompus çà et là par un semis de rimes (comme des fruits défendus au milieu d'un champ d'orties), mais ce ne sont pas encore les climats complètement transposés, la folie des greffes dans les jardins botaniques ou les poèmes jadis versifiés. J'y retrouve cependant la jachère du purgatoire, qui précédait dans l'enfance des paradis de langue vulgaire: à la fraîche une floraison noire de métaphores, une forêt basse abritant le songe d'un grand livre littéral, ouvert sur la «fleur» d'une autre forêt, la *selva oscura* de ce que je ne sais pas nommer.

(Par la fenêtre du solstice, on voit se consumer les restes diurnes des répétitions, dans le petit bois de laurier, de lierre et de buis – *laurus nobili* et tout le reste, prêt à retourner dans le terreau d'une langue vraiment morte.)

. . . .

Aujourd'hui que le récit ne prend plus, il nous reste l'entière nomination: de Linné à Littré l'étymologie fourchue de chaque mot puis une floraison de fleurs mâles et de noms féminins (comme la linnée boréale aux fleurs blanches et penchées, veinées de rouge au-dedans, dont Littré se faisait des tisanes); vétérinaire horticulteur il nous reste tant de litanies, tous les proverbes et les plantes médicinales, et plus de cent phrases à finir dans le latin de l'imaginaire...

Il nous reste à visiter la chambre du lecteur (couvre-lit de marceline et draps de batiste, la commode où l'étoffe est prise

We turn the page, and behind a giant letter (is it the ornate initial letter of a story in regular prose, the flowering tree hiding the forest of an illegible blazon where a sign copied out wrong can still be deciphered beneath the remorse and hesitations of the copyist: some ancient slip of spelling, a mistake in the civil records, in short everything that reminds us of the illusions of memory, the shame of a child, and the recollection of the names we fear losing all the same?) we can see the meadows of sleep where the slumbering author has started to translate in his dream before being woken up by the echo of really scary prophecies. Like a sleepwalker he begins his evening journey again through the monuments of the passion that mix the universal in the involuntary: an ideal palace, a parched garden, a glass house, and chinoiseries or rococo villas placed there amongst the cabbages, the rocks and the mirror-like rivers – a whole apparent disorder where the forgotten tools of prose are left lying around.

Further on the spread-out carpets of the market gardens, interrupted here and there by a scattering of rhymes (like forbidden fruit in the middle of a field of nettles), but these are not yet climes completely transposed, mad grafts onto botanical gardens or poems that were once versified. Nevertheless, there I discover the fallow field of purgatory which in childhood preceded paradises of the vernacular: in the twilight coolness a black flowering of metaphors, a low forest sheltering the dream of a great literal book open at the flower of another forest, the *selva oscura* of what I cannot name.

(Through the window of the solstice we see the diurnal remains of the repetitions and rehearsals being consumed in the little wood of laurel, ivy and beech – *laurus nobili* and all the rest, ready to return to the compost of a truly dead language.)

· ·

Now that story-telling no longer catches on we are left with the entirety of nomination: from Linné to Littré the forked etymology of each word then a flowering of male flowers and feminine names (like the linnaea borealis with its white stooping flowers, red-veined in the middle from which Littré made his tea); horticultural veterinarian we are left with so many litanies, all the proverbs and medicinal plants and more than a hundred sentences to finish in the Latin of the imaginary...

Our last job is to visit the reader's bedroom (marceline bedspread and batiste sheets, the chest with material caught in the crack of

dans la fente des tiroirs, et la carafe qu'on craint de renverser...).
Narcisse toute la nuit regarde passer les bois flottants d'un théâtre:
l'ébène et l'acajou sur les eaux de la mémoire, le bois mort dans le
ru des latrines; le dormeur remonte alors les eaux claires et noires
d'une rivière – le lit mouillé d'un enfant. Qui dans le rêve suivant
(*le sommeil d'amour dure encore*) découvre en même temps que sa
propre image les bâtons brisés de l'écriture.

the drawers, and the water-jug you're afraid to knock over...). All night long Narcissus watches the logs of a theatre floating pass: ebony and mahogany on the waters of memory, dead wood in the stream of the latrines; the sleeper then works back up the clear black waters of a river – the wet bed of a child. Who in the following dream (*the sleep of love goes on*) discovers along with his own image the broken sticks of writing.

L'annonciation

Riche du seul argent volé en rêve et cherchant au poème une raison étrange il me manque toujours le quart de la somme (et les quelques mots d'une devise) pour payer au tourniquet la carte postale déjà écrite. «Vous payerez un peu plus cher», m'avait pourtant prévenu la vendeuse.

On voit encore au verso le vieil or et l'auréole des annonciations: la vierge de trois quarts et l'ange toujours de profil; une chambre à ciel ouvert et le couvre-lit souvent rouge; le souvenir d'un verger et le sens incertain d'une parole portée par le vent, rapportée par les nuages (on entend d'ici le latin du ciel et l'allitération des oiseaux); une scène où s'échangent des mots imprononçables, une injure à l'oreille de l'autre ou le prénom de Joseph absent sous les portiques Renaissance.

Avec les tourments du copiste (trois jours de purgatoire pour une lettre manquée) me reviennent les mots écorchés de ma première faute (j'avais écrit *la née dernière*) et le souvenir retrouvé d'une sœur qui vient de naître. Comme on voit au musée les mots d'une orthographe aujourd'hui étrangère (latin d'église en lettres gothiques), ceux de l'ange aux ailes repliées, qui parle comme un livre pour dire à l'oreille de la vierge la venue d'un enfant futur.

Serinée d'aussi loin la vérité qui souffle encore insinue ses médisances, et dans le nom du père bat le rappel d'un prénom féminin: Léon Joseph Marie, je rapporte à son insu un récit mort sur ses lèvres: quel âge avait-il aux noces de sa mère, quand il portait dans le cortège un baigneur emmailloté, l'enfant de la faute qu'il fallait montrer à la foule, lui-même l'enfant reconnu qu'il dut porter dans les langes, et pencher comme une fille aux fonts baptismaux – miroir d'un peu de ciel et d'une histoire qui se refuse.

Comme au «rendez-moi ça» je reprends la fausse monnaie du commentaire, et réclame un peu d'or pour réchauffer ma folie froide et l'hiver sur les langues mortes. Leur sourdine étouffe les souris du chant, les souvenirs d'une cantatrice et sa voix où s'évanouit le sens, quand elle monte affolée sur le rebord de la scène – ma mère autrefois sur un tabouret de cuisine, apeurée par des souris trop réelles (enceinte une seconde fois, elle inonda de pleurs son tablier puis elle couva les oreillons...).

The Annunciation

Rich only with the silver stolen in dream and seeking some strange reason for a poem I'm always short a quarter (and the few words for a motto to write in a common currency) of what I need to pay at the check-out for the postcard I've already written. Even though the salesgirl had said: 'that will cost you a little more'.

You can still see on the back the old gold and the halo of the annunciations: the angel always in profile and the virgin looking aside; a room open to the heavens and a coverlet which is often red; the hint of an orchard and the uncertain sense of a word carried on the wind, brought back by the clouds (you can hear from here the Latin of the heavens and the alliteration of the birds); a scene in which unpronounceable words are exchanged, an insult in someone's ear or Joseph's name missing under the Renaissance porticos.

In a copyist's torment (three days of purgatory for missing out a letter) the flayed words of my first mistake come back to me (I had written *last born* instead of *last year*) and the memory regained of a sister's birth. Just as in a museum there are words in a spelling foreign to us today (Church Latin in Gothic script), so the words of the angel with folded wings, who talks like a book quietly telling the Virgin of the coming of a future child.

Drummed into us from just as far truth, still whispering, insinuates its gossip, and in the name of the father calls to arms the memory of a woman's name: Léon Joseph Marie, without his knowing I repeat a tale which died on his lips: how old was he at his mother's wedding, in the procession he carried a doll tightly wrapped in its clothes, the child of the fault the crowd had to see, he was the one, the child the crowd recognised and whom he had to carry himself in his swaddling clothes and tend like a girl at the baptismal fonts – a mirror to a bit of sky and a history untold.

Just like when I say 'that's my change' I pick up the counterfeit coinage of commentary and ask for a little gold to warm up my cold madness and the winter that covers dead languages. Their muffled tones stifle the mice in the song, the memories of a diva and her voice where sense swoons as she walks panic-stricken to the edge of the stage – my mother in days gone by sitting on a kitchen stool, frightened by the mice that were all too real (pregnant for the second time she flooded her apron with tears and started getting mumps...).

L'odeur du lait s'est répandue partout, dans la sente et la ruelle, entre les orties blanches et les bois de lit. Dans la chambre éclairée par l'ampoule de saint Janvier (avant des mois le sang ne coulera plus de ses plaies) un bonnet aux oreilles d'âne est abandonné sur une chaise; et dans le jardin, l'ange qui fait la bête s'éloigne sans un mot: accompagné d'un docteur au nom d'oracle il croise une sage-femme, et fait semblant de ne pas voir Joseph dans un coin qui tend des pièges à rats.

The smell of milk has spread everywhere, in the path and the alley, between the white dead-nettles and the bedstead wood. In the room lit by the lamp of St January (for months blood will not flow from his wounds) a cap with ass's ears is left lying on a chair; and in the garden, the angel playing the fool moves away without a word: accompanied by a doctor with an oracular name, he meets a midwife and pretends not to see Joseph in a corner setting rat-traps.

Tête-bêche

Au bord du chemin qui menait jadis à un palais dont le toit s'est effondré, deux enfants nés le même jour jouent aux osselets, à la grenouille, aux épingles, à pigeon vole, et dans le sommeil à pas de géant reconnaissent l'ombre agrandie d'un roi. Roi mage en personne qui vient de traverser le jour et son désert, comme un rêve après l'oubli nous revient chargé de présents.

Le premier est le fils d'une marâtre trop aimante, qui d'un crapaud voulut faire un prince à l'étroit dans son rêve, trop serré dans son habit froncé à la taille. C'est de lui que je tiens, par un étrange héritage, la camisole et le corset, la toise qu'on impose à l'enfance, mais aussi *l'obnubilation des tissus* et le goût de la citation.

L'autre a plutôt honte de ses vêtements trop larges: pour ce Gribouille qui commence à écrire, la promesse faite au langage est déjà une dette qui s'accumule. Et devant le casino trop clair où tourne la chance comme une chouette aveuglée, à cent lieues de tout château à l'intérieur des terres (le château de la naissance où les parents sont emmurés), lui revient le sentiment qu'éprouva peut-être Joseph K devant le gardien qui l'empêchait de frapper à la porte: le sentiment d'être «enfermé dehors».

Leurs pères sont ces hommes, valets de ferme ou rois sans couronne, pour qui le destin n'a pas plus de sens que la manille ou la coinchée du dimanche. Dans l'air penché de Lahire, le profil de Pallas, le nom de Lancelot, la fleur que Rachel respire, un lettré d'un autre continent verrait peut-être une allégorie des saisons et des divinités agraires (ou dans ces figures biseautées comme un miroir, séparées par le tranchant de la guillotine, une histoire illustrée de supplices et de décollations), mais pour les joueurs attablés au cabaret ce ne sont que des personnages tête-bêche qu'ils ordonnent en un précaire éventail (derrière lequel ils ne parviennent pas à cacher leurs yeux rougis par la fatigue et la fumée), rien d'autre que des tierces, des quintes et de possibles atouts. Les noms qu'ils ignorent (et Frogier les ferait peut-être rire, s'il n'est pas sûr qu'Argine les ferait rêver) sont étalés devant eux sans qu'ils songent à les lire, car la lampe qui les éclaire leur permet avant tout de surveiller du coin de l'oeil le voisin qui pourrait tricher.

Top-to-Tail

At the side of a path which once led to a palace whose roof has now collapsed, two children born on the same day are playing jacks, toss the coin, pin the donkey and Simon says, and in the giant footsteps of sleep they recognise the enlarged shadow of a king. A magus in person who has just crossed daylight and his own deserts, as a dream once forgotten comes back to us loaded with presents.

The first is the son of a bad mother with too much love who wanted to take a frog and make a prince trussed up in his dream, all tight in his frock coat gathered angrily at the waist. It is from him, by a strange inheritance, that I've acquired the straitjacket and corset, the yardstick imposed on childhood, but also *an obsession with fabrics* and a taste for quotation.

The other is rather ashamed of his clothes that are too big for him: for that Fool starting to write, the promise made to language is already a growing debt. And in front of the all-too-bright casino where the wheel of fortune turns like an owl blinded by the light, a hundred miles from any castle nestling in its grounds (a birthplace where parents are immured), suddenly he feels again as Josef K did, perhaps, faced with the warden who stopped him from knocking on the gate: the feeling of being 'locked in outside'.

Their fathers are amongst those farmhands or kings without crowns for whom destiny has no more meaning than cards or the Sunday game. In La Hire pouring over his charts, in the profile of Pallas, in the name of Lancelot or the flower that Rachel smells, a person of letters from another continent might have seen an allegory of the seasons and the agrarian gods (or in those faces bevelled like the edges of a mirror, separated from each other by the blade of the guillotine they might also have seen an illustrated history of torture and decapitation), but for the players at the inn these are only top-to-tail figures which they organise in a precarious fan (behind which they fail to hide their eyes reddened by fatigue and smoke), nothing more than threes and fives and possible trumps. Names they do not know (and Frogier might make them laugh if he wasn't sure that Argine would make them wonder) are spread in front of them and they never think to read them, the light from the lamp is just bright enough to look sideways at the next player who might be cheating.

À la pacotille et aux étoiles, à la nuit de Noël ils préfèrent les jours de foire, la roue de la fortune qui ralentit en grinçant comme une charrette à l'essieu rompu au tournant du siècle, les filles un peu grasses et les roses marchandises, et surtout Pierrot dans ses dentelles quand il fait le tour de la ville en chevauchant un cochon.

Quant au pauvre Saturnin, s'il se promène avec des dessous qui font rire, c'est que sa grand'mère a féminisé tous les hommes de la famille. Un jour de son enfance, comme d'autres se lèvent et parlent en langues, ils s'est dressé sur son lit pour réciter des prières, qu'il savait par cœur sans les avoir apprises, après quoi il est descendu dans la cuisine où il a pleuré de joie en tournant autour de la table, derviche sans le savoir et bientôt promis au pavillon des agités.

Car ébloui par la neige et l'hermine, par une justice du même rouge que les ornements de nos campagnes, il entreprit de refaire à sa majorité, miracle après miracle, ce qui avait été accompli par tous les saints – en commençant par couper le cou à tous les dindons du voisinage.

Out with the cheap-jack and the stars, out with Christmas Eve they'd rather have the fair, the wheel of fortune that grates as it slows down like a turn-of-the-century cart with a broken axle, plump girls, rosy trinkets and above all Pierrot in lace riding around the city on a pig.

As for the poor old Saturnine, the reason he goes around in ridiculous underwear is that his grandmother has feminised all the men in the family. One day in his childhood, as others get up and speak in tongues, he sat up in bed to say prayers which he knew by heart without having learnt them, after which he went down to the kitchen where he cried tears of joy as he ran around the table not knowing he looked just like a dervish, and destined soon for the wing of the mentally disturbed.

Dazzled as he was by the snow and the ermine, by a justice of the same red as our rustic ornaments, he undertook from then to adulthood to repeat, miracle by miracle, everything that had been accomplished by the saints – starting with slitting the throats of all the turkeys in the area.

La leçon d'anatomie

Opéré de quelque grosseur comme en attrapent aussi les garçons, on m'endort sous le masque où le ciel se met à tourner plus vite que l'oubli, plus bleu que le vertige, puis c'est au ralenti que continue le voyage du petit mort presque nu sous sa chemise, d'aile en pavillon par les portes de l'envers et de l'endroit, jusqu'à l'apparition d'Anubis assisté de visages vigilants; coiffeur et manucure, avaleur d'ombres et d'entrailles, ils nettoient les instruments de la chirurgie plus délicats que le fragile outil du littérateur. Puis le confesseur à la bouche impure s'approche du dormeur aveuglé sous la lampe; et l'instant d'après, quatre années de souvenirs plus volatils que l'éther sont devenus la mémoire du souffleur qu'on reconnaît à sa robe noire et qu'on retrouvera lisant sous l'abat-jour.

Après un sommeil dont on revient emmailloté je vois ma mère qui s'éloigne à reculons, derrière la vitre où les vivants la rappellent. Par la porte à tambour elle retourne chez nous, dans la salle à manger envahie par la misère et le philodendron, dans la serre orientée et ses nids à poussière (aujourd'hui encore elle fait le ménage de ma chambre et retourne le lit: de la monnaie tombe de mes poches mais je reste silencieux. Après quoi elle ouvre la boîte à couture et regarde rêveuse le jardin japonais: une femme y marche à pas lents, sur des miroirs où elle ne peut se reconnaître...).

C'est la même année, d'angines et de mélancolie (de calomnies à coup sûr et de mensonges prononcés très doucement) qu'il fallut comme en rêve ouvrir les organes sanglants de la parole, une incision qui précède une suite de souvenirs à l'encre rouge: un lapin qu'on écorche, une poule qu'on saigne au ciseau et ma mère accroupie dans la basse-cour...

Le vrai réveil eut lieu des années plus tard, au théâtre anatomique où l'on visite en tournant la chaire de Galilée, bois branlant de la justice entre les phases de Vénus et la lune qui titube, cathedra de l'univers à l'entrée d'un amphithéâtre où l'etudiant debout s'apprête à voir, aux premières approches de l'Inquisition, un cadavre escamoté sous les planches (la grammaire et les mathématiques à la place des livres escamotés eux aussi, quand résonnaient les pas de mon père au tournant de l'escalier – de peur qu'il vienne lire par-dessus mon épaule, entre les lignes où il aurait pu se reconnaître, comme dans l'histoire pourtant vraie de Normand B. qui revient

The Anatomy Lesson

For an operation on the kind of bumps that boys also get, I am put to sleep under the mask and the heavens begin to turn faster than oblivion, bluer than vertigo, then the journey of the tiny corpse, almost naked beneath his shift, continues in slow motion, from wing to ward through the gates of reverse and obverse, right up to the appearance of Anubis assisted by the vigilant faces; hairdresser and manicurist, swallower of shadows and entrails, they clean the surgical instruments more delicate than the fragile tool of the man of letters. And then the confessor with his impure mouth comes towards the sleeper blinded beneath the lamp; and the next moment, four years of memories more volatile than those of the ether have become the memory of the prompter singled out by his black cloak who can always be found reading by the lampshade.

Coming back swaddled from sleep I see my mother backing away to the other side of the window-pane where the living beckon her. Through the revolving door she comes back to our house, into the dining-room invaded by poverty and philodendron, into the greenhouse facing the sun and its dust traps (still today she cleans up my room and turns down the bed: change drops out of my pockets, but I don't say anything. Then she opens the sewing box and looks out dreamily at the Japanese garden: a woman is walking slowly on mirrors in which she cannot see herself...).

In that same year of sore throats and melancholy (of calumnies certainly and lies spoken very softly) as though in a dream the bleeding organs of speech had to be opened up, an incision preceding a flow of memories in red ink: a rabbit being skinned, a chicken being bled with a pair of scissors and my mother squatting in the farm-yard...

The true awakening occurred years later, in the anatomical theatre where visitors can walk around Galileo's rostrum, the shaky wood of justice turned rickety between the phases of Venus and the tottering moon, cathedra of the universe at the entrance of a lecture theatre where the student, with the Inquisition approaching, is standing ready to see a corpse spirited away under the floorboards (grammar and mathematics in place of the books also spirited away when the footsteps of my father rang out on the corner of the stairs – for fear that over my shoulder that he might come and read between the lines where he might have seen himself, just like in

113

de chez l'embaumeur: il n'a pas pu pleurer quand son père est mort, mais il entend toujours le bruit de la terre et des quelques cailloux qu'il a jetés sur le cercueil; il sent en lui le remords et les progrès du scrupule, mais l'embaumeur ne lui a rien dit de ce qu'il voulait savoir: le secret de la sécheresse, des viscères dans les vases, du parchemin et surtout de la feuille d'or sur laquelle il croit écrire, comme l'auteur qui portait d'une ville à l'autre la maladie de la pierre et le souci de l'étymologie.

the story, in fact the true story of Normand B. coming back from the embalmer: unable to cry at the death of his father, he can still hear the sound of the earth and the few stones he threw onto the coffin; he feels remorse and the qualms of conscience rising within him, but the embalmer would tell him nothing he wanted to know: the secrets of the drought, the viscera in vases, the parchment and above all the gold leaf on which he thinks he is writing, like the author who carried his kidney stones from one city to another and a concern for etymology.

Livre muet

La couverture illustrée du rêve, un champ de boutons d'or en-
luminant la nuit, le souvenir d'un pré en pente et d'un temps qui
précédait de peu l'apprentissage de la lecture – années sans ortho-
graphe et sans chronologie, chrysanthèmes et dahlias simplement
effeuillés dans le pur plaisir de la prononciation: les mots dormaient
dans les livres et les morts au cimetière ne savaient rien de mon
enfance.

À l'ombre de lettres en fleurs j'ai appris à épeler l'alphabet avant
de lire le rêve de l'herbier où le mot *Botanique* est écrit en caractères
gras: bulbe majuscule, oubli cerné d'une écriture qui ressemble à
la mienne, où se dissimule une femme en forêt, ses filles dans la
clairière offertes à la manie du bibliophile.

Un signet rouge et or (le même entre les pages du livre et les
plis de la chair) marque l'endroit où reprend le récit, le milieu du
gué où passer le ruisseau, les méandres autour d'un mot qui manque:
ouï-dire et digressions, retours en arrière comme dans le rêve du
romancier qui voudrait inscrire, sur la tranche usée d'un livre muet,
le cri à peine articulé qu'il arrache à son héroïne, un mot ivre de
voyelles qui résume à lui seul toute une histoire. L'aphasie l'a prise
après l'hiver, elle vit à moitié nue devant une maison rouge en ne
sachant plus rien de l'amant qui l'effarouche (c'est lui qu'on voyait
s'enfoncer au cœur de la forêt); elle a tout oublié des métaphores
de la chaleur et du passage de la Bérésina, et quand on la mène au
bord même de l'oubli, dans un jardin de l'ancienne Seine-et-Oise
que traverse une rivière ou son reflet, sur l'incendie éteint le givre
a déjà tracé les lettres en étoile du mot *adieu*. Foudre au cœur du
froid, césure au cœur de la parole, comment pourrait-elle résister
à la violence entrevue de ses souvenirs? Mais s'il neige sur sa bouche
et sur les rives rapprochées de la mémoire, le sens n'en finit pas
de mourir sur ses lèvres.

Sur le même territoire le lecteur poursuit un autre rêve, et re-
connaît dans un carrefour (s'il n'est pas situé sur la route légendaire
qui mène à Thèbes) les lieux-dits où il a passé le plus clair de son
enfance: la forêt est en lisière d'une invisible ville antique (on la
devine très blanche), et l'atmosphère est celle d'une fête: des dra-
peaux colorés flottent au ciel, et dans l'une des allées passe une foule
de jeunes filles, des «courtisanes» dont on voit de dos les jupes un

Mutus Liber

The illustrated cover of dream, a field of golden buttercups illuminating the night, the memory of a sloping meadow and of a time just before the apprenticeship of reading – years without spelling and without dates, chrysanthemums and dahlias simply stripped of their leaves in the pure pleasure of pronouncing: words slept in books and the dead in the cemetery knew nothing of my childhood. In the budding grove of letters I learned to spell out the alphabet before I read the dream of the herbarium where the word *Botany* is written in bold; capital corm, oblivion ringed with a writing that looks like mine, where a woman is disguised as a forest with her young girls in the clearing ready for a bibliophile's obsession.

A red and gold marker (like in the pages of a book and the folds of your flesh) shows the place where the story picks up again, the middle of the ford over the stream, the meanderings around a missing word: hear-say and digression, flashbacks like those in the dream of a novelist wanting to inscribe, on the worn edge of a silent book, a barely articulated cry that he wrenches from his heroine, a word drunk on vowels capturing the whole story. After the winter she was struck down by aphasia, and lives half-naked in front of a red house knowing nothing any more of the lover who frightens her (he's the one we saw running off into the heart of the forest); she's forgotten everything about the metaphors of warmth and the crossing of the Berezina, and when she is led to the very edge of oblivion, in a garden in what used to be the Seine-et-Oise through which a river flows or its reflection, the frost has already traced in star-shaped letters the word *adieu* on the extinguished fire. Lightning in the heart of cold, caesura in the heart of the word – how could she resist the half-glimpsed violence of her memories? But even if it snows on her mouth and on the banks of the narrowing river of memory, sense dies endlessly on her lips.

On the same territory the reader follows another dream, and recognises in a cross-roads (if it isn't on the legendary road leading to Thebes) the localities where he spent the best part of his childhood: the forest borders an invisible ancient city (very white, in the imagination), and the atmosphere is like a festival: coloured flags float in the sky, and in one of the alleys there is a crowd of young girls passing, 'courtisans', from behind you can

peu relevées. Peut-être en voulant les suivre, mais aussi pour être sûr de retrouver son chemin, le lecteur se retourne et voit alors l'envers des drapeaux, des calicots pâles dont le mutisme ne permet aucun repère. Il est donc obligé de revenir sur ses pas, de tourner la tête pour revoir les couleurs et tâcher de s'en souvenir.

En prenant la plume le lendemain pour écrire au verso de quelques livres, lui revient un article de journal qu'il a lu l'avant-veille ('Le chinois en trois jours... et en silence'), la méthode intitulée *the silent way* et les rectangles colorés qui notaient les sons des langues étrangères. Il revoit alors le livre muet qu'il a rêvé, puis les couleurs et les sons qui se répondaient, dans les abécédaires de jadis et les sonnets aux rimes embrassées.

see their skirts are slightly raised. Perhaps because he wants to follow them, but also to be sure of finding his way, the reader turns round and sees the backs of the flags, faded calico whose muteness provides no guiding mark. So he has to retrace his steps, look back to see the colours again and try to remember them.

Picking up his pen the next day to write on the back of some books, a newspaper article he read the day before comes to mind ('Chinese in three days...and in silence'), the method known as *the silent way* and the coloured rectangles which were the notation of foreign languages and their sounds. At that moment he sees the mute book he saw before in a dream, then the colours and sounds in mutual response, in the spelling-books of long ago and the sonnets with enclosed rhymes.

La nature aux abois

Paravent grand ouvert entre le jour et la nuit, or et violet le manuscrit déroulé suit le cours d'une rivière – l'eau troublée du langage et les affluents de la fable, un loup en amont du murmure: l'histoire est plus vieille que l'invention des caractères, et c'est sur les lèvres des femmes qu'il faut suivre ce récit sans commencement.

La source loin des hommes taciturnes, peut-être un baquet où tombaient l'étoile et le sel, un météore évaporé, les souvenirs du baptême et de la toilette – entre l'Oise et l'Huisne l'écho quelquefois inaudible du patois traversant les pays d'ouest.

Confluent au creux de la main, les eaux du mariage se mêlent un peu plus tard en épousant la pente du réel: un jour de neige mes parents en toilette du dimanche, robe noire et costume trempé dans le sang. Nul endroit où s'asseoir en cette vie, drôle de guerre et petits métiers, des heures à genoux au bord du lavoir, pour laver le linge du beau monde dont les initiales et les dentelles ne cachent pas la nudité.

En épelant l'alphabet reviennent les noms que j'avais laissés derrière moi pour être sûr de retrouver la maison des morts: Annezo, Santhune, Bilgris, Réguéda, Sainte-Beuve et Labrunie plus au nord, autant de fantômes en chemises qui se lèvent plusieurs fois la nuit sans réussir à hanter la campagne alentour dont je ne connais ni le latin ni le patois, mais la ciguë qu'on donne à boire au philosophe, le bruit de la crécelle et celui de la faux. Triste lévitation du rêve dont il reste au lever du jour le vertige et le souvenir de l'envol – jusqu'au soir un crapaud sur le cœur, au bord d'une rivière que ne couvre pas le bruit de la lecture.

Aucun livre de chevet pour dire le lendemain l'enluminure et l'ivoire, l'ortie et le tabac, les dominos jusqu'à minuit et l'insomnie d'Éros. Veuvage de l'enfance en tablier noir, vacances entre les draps dans un pays pas plus grand qu'un carré en jachère: l'armoire à glace au bord de la prairie, la glace accrochée au-dehors qui ne méritait pas le nom de miroir (l'aïeule se coiffait au-dessus de l'eau froide) n'ont jamais réfléchi de château ni le regard des trois filles dans la chambre du fond – mais comme un journalier cherchant asile pour la nuit la silhouette du roi Lear et l'invisible qui nous frôle: la chauve-souris qui se prend aux cheveux, l'aile d'un ange qu'on plume avec la volaille.

Nature at Bay

A screen wide open between day and night; gold and violet, the unscrolled manuscript follows the course of a river – the muddied waters of language and the affluents of fable, a wolf upstream from the babbling: the story is older than the invention of letters, and this narrative with no beginning must be followed on the lips of women.

The source now far from taciturn men, perhaps a tub that star and salt fell into, an evaporated meteor, memories of baptism and baths – between the Oise and the Huisne the echo, sometimes inaudible, of the patois crossing the western regions.

Converging in the palm of the hand, later the waters of marriage mingle and wed the slope of the real: a snowy day, my parents in their Sunday best, black dress and suit dipped in blood. Nowhere to sit in this life, funny old war and small-time crafts, hours kneeling beside the wash-tub washing the linen of the gentry, their nakedness hidden by neither the initials nor the lace.

As I spell out the alphabet the names come back to me that I had left behind to be sure of finding my way back to the house of the dead: Annezo, Santhune, Bilgris, Regueda, Sainte-Beuve and Labrunie further north, so many phantoms in shifts who get up several times a night without managing to haunt the surrounding countryside whose patois is all Greek to me, but what I know is the hemlock given to the philosopher, the noises of the rattle and the scythe. A sorry levitation of dream at daybreak, only vertigo and the memory and of taking wing – a toad on the heart until evening, by a river that the noise of reading doesn't drown.

No bedside book next day to tell the illumination and the ivory, nettle and tobacco, dominoes until midnight and the sleepless nights of Eros. The widowing of childhood in a black apron, holidays between the sheets in a country no larger than a tiny field lying fallow; the wardrobe with mirrored doors on the edge of the meadow, the looking-glass hardly worth the name hanging on the outside (the great grand-mother did her hair looking into the cold water) never reflected a castle nor the gaze of the three girls in the back bedroom – but like a daily labourer seeking shelter for the night the silhouette of King Lear and the invisible things which brush against us: the bat catching in the hair, the angel's wing plucked with the poultry.

Entre la basse-cour et l'écurie, dans la bouche bée d'un enfant manque le nom d'une étoile. Plus tard un bibelot sur une étagère de cuisine, et dans l'arrangement d'un bouquet les senteurs de l'absente. Après quoi la phrase ne peut plus rouler que dans l'ornière, comme la tête coupée d'un Baptiste au creux d'un tablier.

Between the farmyard and the stables, in the open mouth of a child the name of a star goes missing. Later some knick-knack on a kitchen shelf, and in some flower arrangement the fragrant aroma of she who is absent. After which the sentence can only roll in the rut, like the severed head of a Baptist in the folds of an apron.

Portrait du donateur

Revivant dans l'aphasie sa chasteté de fille et le châtiment de saint Jérôme, il remue des cendres en se plaignant du mot «jour» (et de son propre nom qu'il entend en deux mots); las de méditer son livre dont la nature même serait jalouse, il estime en avare l'argenterie du mariage et l'or de la virginité, répétant une histoire où les mots de liaison manqueront toujours, s'écriant à part lui «la prononciation restituée», quand il a oublié jusqu'à son vœu de silence, et que délié de sa promesse il ne sait plus pourquoi il a voulu ressembler à ce perroquet au milieu de voix mortes.

En remuant les cendres qu'il tisonne un peu distrait, perdu dans le noir d'un théâtre où sa voix va bientôt s'éteindre, il se plaint dans le mot «nuit» du cuivre des voyelles, de la sonnette et du marteau, des coups redoublés qui heurtent la raison...

La rivière à ses pieds qui cherche une embouchure en des ruisseaux de rien (il se revoit à minuit, pieds nus sur le carreau de la cuisine, et la sensation du froid lui revient quand une femme l'a surpris), la rivière se confond avec le flot de paroles qui finira sur ses lèvres en un mince filet de sang.

Depuis trente ans qu'il ne fait plus le geste d'écrire, je crains encore son jugement dans les marges, et quand il se retourne vers nous (mon père m'accompagne: jaloux depuis longtemps de la tête édentée dont je parle beaucoup trop, il a tenu à visiter avec moi la maison natale), quand ce vieil enfant aveuglé se retourne vers nous je vois dans son œil une aiguille d'or, l'agrafe qui fermait le vêtement maternel, et je sais pour m'en souvenir qu'il a la vision de deux femmes: la mère est une veuve un peu bretonnante et elle attend la mort, la fille trop maquillée n'a pas encore de mari...

Pauvre volatile dont le cri se résout en douleur à hauteur du bréchet, il se croit guéri de la gorge dont on ne guérit jamais, et murmure les prénoms d'une famille illégitime; puis il nous montre sur un vieil almanach le phénix et l'infante défunte, mais je devine la gêne et la rougeur de mon père qui ne voit que l'œil idiot d'un gallinacé dans cette image déjà jaunie.

Nous repartons par le même sentier que jadis, à travers des fables et des forêts marquées de pierres blanches, de mots oubliés qui cognent à la vitre après minuit, quand l'enfant prodigue va se mettre à parler – mais l'orphelin étouffe un cri en découvrant la maison vide, et la couronne sur le crâne de son père, ce roi de

Portrait of the Donor

Reliving in aphasia his girlish chastity and the punishment of Saint Jerome, he stirs the ashes and complains of the word 'daylight' (and of his own name which he hears as two words); weary of meditating on his book, of which nature itself would be jealous, like a miser he counts up the silver of marriage and the gold of virginity, reiterating a story where the link-words will always be missing, crying out quietly 'pronunciation restored' when in fact he has forgotten even his vow of silence and absolved of his promise, he no longer knows why he wanted to be like that parrot in the midst of dead voices.

Stirring and fanning the ashes a little distractedly, lost in the darkness of a theatre where his voice will soon be extinguished, he complains of the brass vowels in the word 'night', about the bell and the hammer, the repeated blows that man-handle reason...

The river at his feet seeking an outlet in meagre rivulets (he can see himself at midnight barefoot on the kitchen tiles, and that feeling of coldness comes back that he got when a woman took him by surprise), the river merges with the flow of words which will finish up on his lips as a thin trickle of blood.

In the thirty years since he took up a pen, I still fear his judgements in the margin, and when he turns to us (my father is with me: long since jealous of the toothless head I speak of far too much, he has insisted on coming with me to visit the house where I was born), when this overgrown, blinded child turns to us I can see a gold needle in his eye, the fastening on the maternal garment, and I know because I can remember that he has the vision of two women: the mother is a widow sounding a bit Breton and waiting for death, the daughter has too much make-up and still no husband...

Poor fowl whose cry comes up at the wishbone as pain, he thinks himself cured of the ailing throat that has no cure, and murmurs the forenames of an illegitimate family; then shows us the phoenix and the late infanta in an old almanac, but I can guess at the embarrassment and the blushes of my father who can only see the vacant eye of a gallinacean in this photograph that has already turned yellow.

We leave by the same path as in days gone by, through fables and forests marked with white stones, with dead words knocking at the window after midnight when the prodigal child is getting ready to speak – but the orphan stifles a scream seeing the empty house and the crown on the skull of his father, that necropolis

nécropole qui mendiait au carrefour...

Traversant le cimetière où les tombes sont ouvertes, j'entends derrière moi le bruit d'un corps trop lourd qui trébuche en terre, et quand je vois venir à ma rencontre Œdipe et les deux larrons en costumes de mariés, je comprends mais trop tard les mots d'une ancienne prophétie, comme on entend une rime trop sonore à la fin d'un mauvais rêve.

king begging at the crossroads...

Crossing the cemetery with its open tombs, I can hear the noise behind me of a heavy body stumbling into the ground, and when I see Oedipus and the two thieves in bridegroom suits coming towards me, I understand, too late, the words of an ancient prophecy, like a ponderous rhyme at the end of a bad dream.

Un détail de l'enfer

I

C'est toujours donnant donnant à l'entrée des bibliothèques, où livré à un autre soi-même on vous conduit jusqu'à la salle des pas perdus. «Vous passerez d'abord sous une porte dorée», m'avait-on promis, mais je n'ai le souvenir que du bois vermoulu, des trois marches et du long corridor qu'il fallait parcourir sans se retourner, sous l'œil sans regard des lecteurs, malgré la consigne de se taire continuant à chuchoter les patenôtres des morts – la messe basse des mots que je savais par cœur avant qu'on me donne un livre pour un autre, un manuscrit enluminé de silences au lieu d'un récit noir sur blanc.

Pendant qu'un enfant compte sur ses doigts pour trouver douze avant de se perdre dans les lignes de la prose, à travers la salle des catalogues on me conduit par une porte dérobée jusqu'à la loge de l'enfer. Devant un miroir et une chaise vide (le miroir où Angèle V. perdit la vue, aveuglée par le lac rouge au milieu du salon), l'auteur qui signait de ses initiales et qui ne livra rien de son vivant, s'apprête à lire ou plutôt à jeter du fond d'un naufrage, comme s'il avait devant lui la partition du *Déluge,* une phrase qui roule sans point ni virgule en suivant le parcours des étoiles, le long d'un grand in-folio dont il tourne les pages sans même les regarder: on sent dans sa voix l'hiver intime et la passion qu'il a toujours mise à éviter le récit, la narration trop claire où il achèverait de perdre sa *petite raison virile*…

Dans la tisane étoilée qu'il buvait après minuit se reflète en tremblant la folie d'un autre: Littré quand il entrevoit dans un seul verbe une fleur prête à tomber, la tête qu'on tranche et quelques mots qui se détachent – la rose contrariée, la violette et le balbutiement, liste jamais close qui continue à voler sur d'autres lèvres. Condamnées à l'écho pour n'avoir pas su aimer, leur murmure est si mince qu'on a cru l'enfermer dans le corset étroit de quelques voyelles.

A Detail from Hell

I

You give as good as you get at library entrances; you are led to the hall of lost footsteps by another you. 'First you go through a gilded doorway,' I had been promised, but my only memory is of worm-eaten wood, the three steps and the long corridor you had to walk down without looking back under the gazeless eyes of the readers who, in spite of the instruction to keep quiet, continue whispering the paternosters of the dead – the low mass of words I already knew by heart at the moment I was given one book for another, a manuscript illuminated with silences in place of a story in black and white.

In the time that it takes a child to count out twelve syllables on his fingers before getting lost in the lines of prose, I am led across the catalogue room and through a concealed door to the lobby of the Forbidden Books Room. In front of a mirror and an empty chair (the mirror in which Angèle V. lost her sight, blinded by the red lake in the middle of the drawing-room), the author who used his initials as a signature and delivered nothing in his lifetime is making ready to read, or rather to cast into a shipwreck, as though he had the score of the *Flood* in front of him, a sentence which rolls along without stop or comma, follows the path of the stars and the length of a large *in-folio* whose pages he turns without looking at them: the winter of his soul comes out in his voice, and the passion he has always put into avoiding storytelling and narrative so clear that he might finally lose his *little virile reason...*

In the starry tea he would drink after midnight there shimmers the reflection of another's madness: Littré glimpsing in a single verb a flower ready to drop, a head being severed and a few words splitting off – the thwarted rose, the violet and the stammer, a never ending list which continues its flight on other lips. Condemned to echo for having failed to love, their murmuring is so tenuous it was thought possible to enclose it in the narrow corset of a few vowels.

II

Par la fenêtre de l'enfer, sur la prairie où pousse avec l'immortelle et la renouée le lierre apporté par Paulhan, on aperçoit la maison de conversation aux volets clos – jadis une volière (de paroles, de hiéroglyphes et de rêves), aujourd'hui une maison de jeu encombrée de tables, où se rend le lecteur qu'on vient d'appeler par son nom, et qui va risquer en silence une dernière mise.

Alors qu'il n'a jamais montré que son visage (et ses mains quand elles dépassaient de l'étoffe aux larges manches), quand il revient à lui c'est pour sortir enfin de la chasteté de l'ombre: il allume la lampe et tourné vers les morts, il peint ses lèvres en bleu avant d'écrire. Le réel à jamais veuf, la voilette peut retomber sur le visage de mon sosie, plus pâle que les souvenirs que j'invente et plus vieux que le parricide.

La porte est battante et je veux m'enfuir, mais une marchande à la toilette me demande des nouvelles de mon père qu'elle a connu valet de chambre (minuit passé, dans le vestibule il attendait le retour des maîtres pour leur ôter leur manteau), puis elle ouvre une armoire à glace où sont suspendus des costumes et des déshabillés d'hiver: sur ce vestiaire qu'on ne peut voir qu'en privé (vêtements d'une ombre ou d'un prince travesti, dernière coquetterie devant la mort) elle veille avec la même jalousie que sur les manuscrits les plus précieux.

«C'est le linge de Lazare», me confie-t-elle comme un secret, mais le linge n'est pas marqué, et je vois Lazare errant à la recherche de son nom, qu'il a oublié après trois jours de sommeil. Ressuscité célibataire il songe aux noces de ses sœurs, et s'enroule comme un enfant dans les draps de son premier lit.

II

Through the window of the Forbidden Room, on the meadow where the everlasting flower and the knotwort grow with the ivy brought in by Paulhan, the house of conversation can be seen with its shutters closed – in days gone by an aviary (of words, of hieroglyphs and dreams), today a gaming house cluttered with tables where the reader turns up when his name is called and places one last bet in silence.

Although he has never shown more than his face (and his hands when they protruded beyond the material with the wide sleeves), when he comes round he finally leaves the chastity of the shadows: he lights the lamp and, turned towards the dead, paints his lips blue before starting to write. The real now forever widowed, the veil can fall back over the face of my double, paler than the memories I invent and more ancient than parricide.

The door is banging and I want to flee, but a woman selling second-hand fineries asks about my father whom she knew as a valet (past midnight, he would wait for the masters' return to take their coats), then she opens a mirrored wardrobe with winter suits and negligées: she watches over this cloakroom seen only in private (clothes of a shadow or a transvestite prince, a last moment of coquettishness before death) with the same jealousy as over the most precious manuscripts.

'It's Lazarus's laundry,' she confides to me as though it were a secret, but the laundry is not marked and I see Lazarus wandering in search of his name, which he has forgotten after three days' sleep. A bachelor raised from the dead, he dreams of his sisters' weddings and rolls like a child in the sheets of his first bed.

L'enfant prodigue

Enfants de plusieurs lits nous avons volé nos noms sur les lèvres des morts – les aînés de père inconnu, les filles au défaut héréditaire qui boitent en attendant le mariage, avatars d'un rêve illustre écrit à l'heure où se réveille une femme insultée. Elle ne dira rien des secrets de la filiation ni de la bâtardise du genre humain, ce croisement du rossignol et du crapaud qui bâtit des théâtres pour chanter. Ou pour couvrir une voix qui jargonne, mêlant le parler gallo et l'argot des jardins, les ronces et le liseron jamais fleuri s'enroulant autour d'une «branche mère».

Le goût du lait revient en parlant, le lait caillé dans les bols quand la lune rousse éclairait la faïence et l'eau qui dort. À l'intérieur d'une maison sans feu le sommeil est troublé par *les soupirs de la sainte et les cris de la fée*, par la chute au pied du lit des vêtements de la femme adultère. Sa voix dans les livres se confond avec une ancienne désinence, une langue jamais apprise qui revient à l'oreille de l'enfant. Rougeurs et silences qui précèdent un flot de paroles et leur contraire, un mascaret d'émotions qui remonte en même temps que la mémoire et la marée.

Si l'enfant prodigue et saturnien éclate en sanglots (le vendredi maigre où il revient), c'est encore à cause de l'amour qu'on lui montre du doigt. L'anneau de sa mère enferme à jamais les larmes de son corps, l'anguille et la rivière plus vif-argent que ses souvenirs.

Accompagné du vautour qu'on croyait femelle et fécondé par le vent, quand il repart c'est pour trouver le partage des eaux; entre la sanglante et l'amoureuse, la rose et les ténèbres, la rime et le bruit... Héros roturier il apprend à écrire en prose, mais lit les vers en se taisant pour mieux entendre en lui *l'instrument des tristes*, et l'accent de la superstition quand ils parlent de l'avenir (leur histoire est sans écriture et sans roi, leur voix est en souffrance dans les voyelles trop fermées de l'alphabet).

Comme la parole et l'écho la maison du père est divisée depuis toujours. Foudre et cerisier ne répondent pas au même nom, et dans la chambre où frère et sœur se déshabillent, même les jumeaux ne se ressemblent pas.

The Prodigal Son

Children born of several beds we have stolen our names on the lips of the dead – the older brothers born of an unknown father, daughters with hereditary defects limping as they wait to be married off, avatars of an illustrious dream written when an affronted wife awakens. She will say nothing of the secrets of lineage, nor of the bastardy of the human race, that crossing of the nightingale with the toad which builds theatres in which to sing; or to cover up a jabbering voice, mingling Gallic with garden slang, briar with bindweed that never flowered and wraps itself around a "feeding branch".

The taste of milk comes back as we speak, the curdled milk in the bowls when the ruddy moon lit up the crockery and the sleeping water. Inside a house without a fire sleep is disturbed by *the sighs of the saint and the cries of the fairy*, by the clothes of the adulterous wife falling at the foot of the bed. Her voice in books is lost in an ancient inflexion, a language which has never been learned and which comes back to the ears of the child. Blushes and silences preceding a stream of words and their opposite, a tidal wave of emotions heaving with memory and the tides.

If the prodigal and Saturnine child bursts into tears (on the fasting Friday of his return), it is still for love that the finger points to him. His mother's ring encloses his body's tears forever, and the eel, and the river more quick-silver than his memories.

With the vulture thought to be female and fertilised by the wind, when he leaves it will be to find the parting of the waters; between the bleeding and the loving, the rose and the darkness, rhyme and noise... A common hero, he learns to write in prose but keeps quiet reading the verse, the better to hear within him *the instrument of the unhappy*, and the accent of superstition when the unhappy speak of the future (their story is unwritten and unruled, its voice in abeyance in the over-enclosed vowels of the alphabet).

Like word and echo, the house of the father has been forever divided. Lightning and cherry tree do not answer to the same name, and in the room where brother and sister undress even twins are not alike.

Rouge et or

Le livre ouvert de lui-même au passage de la mer rouge, or sur la tranche et vent de sable à la lisière, la désinence ébruitée dans la voix du désir (le nom de la tribu, tambour à l'oreille de l'enfant): toujours sans musique, et sourd au vocatif, j'avais le pressentiment de mots sans voyelles, et d'un secret trop lourd à porter pour un père aux prénoms imprononçables: Léon né à l'envers, Joseph aux oreilles d'âne, Marie enceinte encore une fois.

Rêvant de la maigreur de l'orphelin, dans mes dégoûts j'inventais des interdits alimentaires, *fêtes de la faim* pour répondre au silence – et la monotone littérature, rime et refrain pour étouffer l'idolâtrie, me disait les testaments mêlés comme les eaux de fleuves aux grossières embouchures: la Vilaine et le Jourdain, la Vivonne et les affluents d'Anna Livia, sans compter les doubles consonnes que roulent tant de rivières et de prénoms féminins: désert inondé, déluge de sensations…

La terre livresque se souvient d'un soleil jaune, de l'aurore fourrée, de l'étoile au-dessus du magasin de mode et de lettres à traduire sur lesquelles se penche un enfant bientôt myope. Bâtons brisés l'écriture lui faisait mal, et la souffrance est encore sans nom quand il s'agit d'enlacer les lettres l'une à l'autre, pour errer sans retour dans une forêt sans paroles.

Provision de bois pour l'hiver, je trace avec les traits de l'oubli des lettres capitales, en souvenir d'une opération vieille comme le monde: chirurgie légère de la mémoire, c'est à la craie rouge qu'on en marquait la cicatrice, comme on inscrivait les rubriques en haut des livres, – quelques majuscules où je relis aujourd'hui l'énoncé de mes hantises: l'E dans l'O des oracles et des accouplements contre nature, le H qu'on prononce encore en certains endroits, les deux consonnes pour désigner le meurtrier d'un dieu, le bois de lit et l'oreiller qui ne doivent pas se toucher, la coupe et l'enjambement, les brèves et les longues d'une langue morte, le doigt mouillé de Lazare tournant les pages d'un livre à venir, les voyelles absentes dans les mille et les cent des chiffres romains…

Dans ces marques de tâcheron je reconnais le nom de l'homme: d'Égypte en Judée le nom changeant d'Œdipe, et dans quatre initiales retrouvées grâce à une rime, I.N.R.I., le prénom d'Irène et l'interdit tacitement signifié. E muet de l'amour dont le dieu est orné d'une verge inutile, ce «jésus» qui prête à rire comme tant d'autres petits noms.

Red and Gold

The book fallen open at the crossing of the Red Sea, gold on the edge and desert wind on the border, the inflexion noised abroad in the voice of desire (the name of tribe, drum at the child's ear): always without musicality and deaf to the vocative, I had a premonition of words without vowels and a secret too heavy to be carried by a father with unpronounceable forenames: Léon born backwards, Joseph with ass's ears, Mary pregnant again.

Dreaming of the orphan's skinniness, in my moments of nausea I invented alimentary taboos, *feasts of starvation* as an antidote to silence – and monotonous literature, with rhyme and refrain to stifle idolatry, spoke the old and new testaments to me mixed together like rivers with wide mouths: the Vilaine and the Jordan, the Vivonne and the affluents of Anna Livia, not counting the double consonants rolled on so many rivers and women's forenames: desert flood, deluge of sensations...

The bookish earth remembers a yellow sun, the stuffed-up dawn, the star above the fashion store and letters for translation that a child is pouring over, short-sighted before long. Aimless writing used to hurt him, and the nameless pain endures when it comes to joining up one letter to the next just to wander with no return in a forest without words.

Supply of wood for the winter I trace these capital letters with the strokes of oblivion, in memory of an operation as old as the world: minor surgery of the memory, the red scar of it was marked out with chalk in the same way as the headings were inscribed in books, – a few capitals in which today I re-read the utterances of my dread, the E in the O of oracles and unnatural couplings, the H which is still pronounced in some places, the two consonants designating the murderer of a god, the bedpost and the pillow which are not allowed to touch, caesura and enjambement, the short and long syllables of a dead language, the moistened finger of Lazarus turning the pages of a book yet to come, the thousands and hundreds in Roman numerals where the vowels are missing...

In these hack's marks I recognise the name of man: from Egypt to Judea the changes in the name of Oedipus, and in the four initials rediscovered through a rhyme, I.N.R.I., the forename of Irene and the interdiction tacitly signified. The mute E of love whose god is adorned with an extra prong, that little darling who makes you laugh like so many other infant names.

Selva oscura

Laisses au bord de la prairie, sentences au bord de la prose, on s'éloigne à pas lents d'une forêt hiéroglyphique: l'aigle pour la glotte, le hibou pour le murmure, la femme de profil, la vipère à cornes et la demi-lune, le vautour superflu dans le nom de la veuve, l'abeille bleue et les consonnes trop brèves, le souvenir de la voix, l'argile et le roseau avant que la terre devienne un livre, avant les douze chants du déluge et leurs milliers de variantes.

L'écorce et le cœur, le scarabée même font partie d'une forêt plus réelle: bois de taille et de corvée, *saoulerie de palmes* et de réminiscences, tout ce qui revient vers nous par le sentier des petites coutumes, avant qu'un écolier marque en traits rouges les arbres abattus sur le livre des comptes. Il entend en lui la voix de sourd qui comptait par six ou par trois le bétail et les graines, et voit briller dans un tiroir, avec l'ongle doré des morts, les lunettes empruntées au maître. Mais nul instrument pour mesurer l'invisible quart de tour de l'écriture.

Coiffe et résille, veste de velours et vérité «mangée aux rats», un mot vient alors à manquer comme une maille emportant tout l'ouvrage, où des mains de femme ont cousu les nombres et des lettres d'or, – la mémoire des lettrés qui comptent leurs pas jusqu'à l'éclipse, somnambules cherchant à deviner, dans l'air de l'automne ou l'intonation d'une langue ancienne, la légère amnésie que sera leur mort – un jeûne un peu prolongé sur une terre avare dont on entretient le souvenir: rimes et miniatures, orthographe enluminée, autant de rêves de mauvais riches qui n'empêchent pas le cousinage des morts, la parenté de l'ange avec un journalier qui repose à droite en entrant.

Ni la ressemblance de Léonore et d'Eurydice, travesties dans les changements à vue d'un opéra sans voix: Orphée en banlieue ne se retourne plus, mais perdu dans ses souvenirs il dévore du regard une vieille apprivoisant les rats: de jour en jour ils couinent un peu moins fort, comme l'enfant qui voulait étouffer les confidences du père.

Son corps lourd est enfermé dans un mobilier cunéiforme (divan, cercueil et meubles d'angle), toute la menuiserie du sommeil si mal chevillée, que démolit un vieillard à la hache dont je crains en moi la colère.

Selva Oscura

Water-marks and stanza breaks on the edge of the meadow, maxims on the border of prose, slowly we step away from a forest of hieroglyphs: eagle for the glottis, owl for the murmur, woman in profile, horned viper and half-moon, the superfluous vulture within the name of the widow, the blue bee and the consonants that are too short, the memory of voice, clay and reed before earth turns into book, before the twelve songs of the flood and their thousand variants.

Bark and heart, and even the beetle are part of a forest that is more real: work the wood to pay the tax, *bingeing on palm trees* and reminiscences, everything that comes back towards us along the path of tiny customs before a schoolboy with his account book marks in red the trees that have been cut down. He hears within him the deaf voice that used to count cattle and grain in sixes or threes, and sees gleaming in a drawer, along with the gilded claw of the dead, the teacher's spectacles he had borrowed. But no instrument with which to measure the invisible corner into writing.

Head-dress and hair-net, velvet jacket and "rat-gnawed" truth, a word is found missing like a link carrying off the whole work where a woman's hands have sown the numbers and letters of gold – the memory of men of letters counting their steps up to the eclipse, somnambulists seeking to devine, in the Autumn air or the tones of an ancient language, the light amnesia which will be their death – a fast prolonged a little on a miserly earth whose memory we maintain: rhymes and miniatures, illuminated spelling, so many dreams of the bottom-of-the-class rich not without the kinship of the dead, the family ties of the angel and a day labourer lying buried there on the right as you come in.

Nor without the resemblance between Leonora and Eurydice, disguised and changing on demand in a silent opera: the Orpheus of the suburbs no longer looks back, but lost in his memories his gaze devours an old woman taming the rats: day by day they squeal a little less loudly, like the child wanting to stifle what father confided in him.

His heavy body is locked up in cuneiform furniture (sofa, coffin and corner pieces), all the ill-joined carpentry of sleep smashed by an old man with an axe whose anger I fear within me.

La pantoufle de verre

La verrerie, le bal et les voyelles: tout un fragile édifice où les souvenirs voisinent avec les nombres, dont la chute ne serait pas plus sonore, sur le parquet ciré où glissent les sœurs, que la révolution d'un météore après minuit, à l'heure où la souricière va se refermer sur la ménagerie du désir. Les *bêtes de songe* ont quitté leur livrée un instant trop tard, et le naturel reprend ses droits: j'entends son pas dans le couloir jusqu'à ce carreau qui sonnait creux, comme dans le compte des syllabes une rime trop prévue, la voix des revenants dans un refrain sans parole ou ce qu'on emprunte à une langue étrangère pour qualifier d'un mot le rouge et la voix.

Je jure qu'il rôde encore autour d'une maison fermée à double tour (devinant dans une boîte à épices, dans les vases et la pharmacopée les senteurs d'un autre siècle) et qu'au-delà du bois d'or et de cendres où flotte une odeur de lessive il voit de loin Magellan qui déménage, comme à travers une longue-vue les hôtels de la vieille Europe et la passe étroite de la mort: entre le pair et l'impair autant de portes battantes, le chiffre effacé de la chambre et le fétiche d'un enfant receleur: peut-être un bouton de nacre qu'on piétine, un coquillage où se résume le monde – poussière, murmure, et le dimanche un nuage de poudre de riz.

En suivant l'ellipse et l'étoile, orienté par l'amitié des nombres et l'amour des simples, je revois la danse d'une sœur apprenant à marcher, dont le pied tourne et l'entraîne à la renverse. Puis la poésie qui boite en prose, et que ne soutient plus *l'appareil du scribe*, mais un enfant qui commence à écrire, hystérique futur. Les maladies de sa mère le tourmenteront en effet, et l'infirmité d'une ballerine mimant des métamorphoses pour lesquelles elle n'est pas faite: ailes arrachées, sur des chaussures à talons plats elle longe la rampe et le rebord de la fenêtre, réminiscence de la douleur qui finit par s'endormir à mon chevet.

Autour du pied meurtri de la danseuse (quelle Gradiva de douze ou treize ans promise à l'infanticide, ou quelle Cendrillon essayant un soulier d'homme?) les bandelettes qu'on défait se confondent avec les festons de la phrase. Mais je garde pour moi (pour le peu de mémoire à venir, dans les boucles et les nœuds de l'écriture) les aveux de son corps taciturne et l'image du bâton de rouge qu'elle délaya entre ses doigts.

The Glass Slipper

Glasswork, the ball and vowels: a whole fragile edifice where memories rub shoulders with numbers whose collapse onto the polished floor on which the sisters are gliding would make no more noise than a meteor turning on its tail after midnight, when the mouse-trap is about to close on the menagerie of desire. The *beasts of dream* have doffed their livery a moment too late, and real life reclaims its rights: I hear its step in the corridor right up to those floor-tiles which had a false ring like a rhyme coming out too obviously from the metre, like the voice of the ghosts in a wordless refrain or what we borrow from a foreign language to describe, in a single word, rouge and voice.

I swear he is still lurking round a double-locked house (divining in a spice jar, in the vases and in the pharmacopoeia the scents of another century) and that on the other side of the wood of gold and ashes where the smell of washing pervades he can see Magellan from afar moving out, like spying through an eye-glass the hotels of old Europe and the narrow pass of death: so many double doors between the odd- and even-syllabled verses, the worn away room number and the fetish of an underage receiver of stolen goods: perhaps a mother-of-pearl button to kick about, a shell epitomising the world – dust, a murmur, and a hint of face powder on a Sunday.

Following the eclipse and the star, guided by a feeling for numbers and the love of simpletons, I remember the dancing step of a sister learning to walk twisting her foot and falling down backwards. Then poetry limping in prose, no longer supported by *the scribe's apparatus*, but a child beginning to write; an hysteric of the future. His mother's illnesses will certainly torment him, as well as the disability of a ballerina miming metamorphoses for which she is not built: wings torn off, wearing flat-heeled shoes she walks along the footlights and window ledge, a souvenir of pain that in the end drops off to sleep at my bedside.

Around the dancer's bruised foot (what twelve- or thirteen-year-old Gradiva bound for infanticide, or what Cinderella trying on a man's shoe?) the bandages being removed look like the festoons on a sentence. But I keep to myself (for the paucity of memory to come, in the bows and knots of handwriting) the confessions of her taciturn body and the stick of rouge that she thinned down with her fingers.

Pierrot valet de la mort

Comme une dernière parenthèse à cause de la peur de ne plus parler français, l'histoire d'un manuscrit perdu nous mène hors du théâtre où trois soirs de suite le souffleur s'est évanoui. Au même instant toutes les fois: quand l'acteur seul en scène, qui tient le rôle d'un comédien agonisant devant l'armoire aux costumes, va mettre un masque pour mourir, car il sait que Hamlet ne sera jamais personne. Ni Othello, ni Hippolyte, ni d'autres fils qui vont lui survivre, d'autres pères qu'il a cru incarner quand il n'endossait que leurs parures: il se voit maintenant descendre aux oubliettes, prendre la place du souffleur et reposer dans sa fausse mémoire.

Trois fois les spectateurs des loges l'ont vu s'évanouir dans le miroir du fond (quand la fente du rideau s'est agrandie) sans pouvoir décider si cette soudaine absence faisait partie de son muet répertoire, ou s'il était assailli dans son trou par la hantise revenue, le souvenir retrouvé, – par Lazare ou Pierrot venant vers lui sans rire, pour revisiter la maison natale dont il est la pauvre idole et le gardien.

Car tous les soirs il se figurait jouer *Pierrot valet de la mort*, et tournant les pages dans le même silence qu'un enfant pris en faute, il regardait sous la lumière du lucernaire (une foudre oubliée) des acteurs trop sûrs d'eux qui voulaient se souvenir de tout, mais qui n'entendraient jamais rien de la sourdine, en lui, des phrases qui viendraient peut-être à manquer.

Une comédienne a pris le deuil de sa parole, et de sa propre nudité qui va virer de l'or au noir (quand elle était dos tournée, j'essayais aussi les chaussures de ma mère, mais je tombais de ne pouvoir marcher comme elle sur des talons trop hauts. Comme aujourd'hui, l'hiver passée dans le *fauteuil sombre*, quand je voudrais tomber dans le sommeil d'un autre).

Pierrot the valet of death

Like a last parenthesis coming from the fear of no longer speaking French, the story of a lost manuscript carries us away from the theatre where the prompter fainted three nights in a row. At the same moment each time: when the actor alone on the stage, playing the role of an actor dying in front of a wardrobe, is about to put on a mask to die in, for he knows that Hamlet will never be anyone. Nor Othello, nor Hippolytus, nor any other sons who will outlive him, other fathers that he thought to embody when in fact he was only wearing their trappings: now he sees himself going down into the dungeon, taking the place of the prompter and lying buried in that false memory.

Three times the spectators in the boxes saw him faint in the mirror at the back (when the crack in the curtain widened) without knowing whether this sudden blank was part of his mute repertoire, or whether he'd been overcome down in his hole by a return of dread, a memory rediscovered, – by Lazarus or Pierrot coming mirthless towards him to revisit the house where they were born and of which he is the feeble idol and guard.

For each evening he imagined himself playing *Pierrot the valet of death*, and turning the pages in the silence of a child caught in the wrong, he watched under the skylight (a forgotten thunderbolt) over-confident actors trying to remember everything but who would never hear any of the mute playing within him of the sentences that might in the end be missing.

An actress is in mourning for his words, and for her own nakedness veering from gold to black (when she had her back to me, I'd also try on my mother's shoes but I'd fall, couldn't walk like she could in those high heels. Like now, spending the winter in the *dark armchair*, when I'd like to fall into the sleep of someone else).

La forêt qui se met à marcher

Est-ce la forêt qui se met à marcher comme à la fin de *Macbeth,* ou la mort qui s'avance en armure, l'anneau de la sécheresse à son doigt décharné? Dans le sommeil agité de la nature le lièvre est effrayé par le lion, le moineau par l'aigle et l'homme par les têtes couronnées qui dorment comme des souches.

Arthur Meslin ne sait rien de ces forêts livresques, des carrefours en étoile et de la croisée des chemins. Il se souvient seulement des flocons de neige dans lesquels il voyait des fleurs d'obéissance, et des ouvriers vêtus de bleu qui cueillaient des violettes en avril; il se souvient des cavalières en velours noir qui flattaient le col de leurs juments, de leurs jambes qui n'étaient pas comme les siennes arquées par la douleur.

De l'avenir dont il voit le reflet dans un verre à liqueur orné d'un filet d'or, il ne connaît que le destin des assis, l'hiver au coin du poêle, dans la cuisine où le lait déborde, mêlant son odeur à celle de la chique et du tabac refroidi, de l'urine aussi quand il ne peut plus se lever.

Le corps contrefait de sa femme qui se dandine en marchant, et qu'on trouvera inanimée sur le carreau de la cuisine, c'est pour beaucoup plus tard, quand lui-même aura quitté le bout de la table en tremblant comme une feuille. Car la mort ici n'est pas le peu profond ruisseau dont on cherche la source, mais un méchant courant d'air dans le couloir où l'hiver s'engouffre, et qu'il faut traverser pour aller de la cuisine à la chambre.

Le cadavre d'Arthur est le premier que j'ai vu, lavé par des mains rougies d'engelures, – les mains gercées de Gervaise Vidor.

The Forest Is Coming

Is it the forest coming forward like at the end of *Macbeth*, or death coming on in its armour, the ring of drought on his emaciated finger? In nature's troubled sleep the hare is frightened by the lion, the sparrow by the eagle and man by crowned heads sleeping like logs.

Arthur Meslin knows nothing of these bookish forests, of star-shaped cross-roads and the meeting of paths. He remembers only the snow flakes that for him are flowers of obedience, and the workers in blue picking violets in April; he remembers the horse-women in black velvet caressing the necks of their mares, their legs so unlike his own bandied by pain.

Of a future whose reflection he can see in a liqueur glass with a gold filament he sees only the destiny of those who remain seated in winter in the corner by the stove, in the kitchen where the milk is boiling over, its smell combining with the smell of chewing tobacco and stale pipes, and urine as well when he can't get up anymore.

The misshapen body of his wife waddling along, who was later found lifeless on the kitchen tiles, and that is for much later when he himself will have left the head of the table, shaking like a leaf. For here, death is not the shallow stream we hunt the source of, but a wicked draught in the hall where winter rushes in and which you have to cross to get from the kitchen to the bedroom.

Arthur's corpse was the first I ever saw, it had been washed with hands all red from chilblains, – the chapped hands of Gervaise Vidor.

Bois dormant

Château de fougères et *sommeil dans un nid de flammes*, la forêt s'est refermée sur une belle endormie au visage d'ébène, une morte maquillée de vermillon.

Vierge enceinte à son insu, mère du jour et de l'aurore qui la réveilleront bientôt, elle dort sans rêve et sans parole au cœur du livre entrouvert, où l'enfant qui vient d'apprendre à lire la regarde à la dérobée, un doigt sur les lèvres en attendant le baiser sur la bouche.

Il voudrait apprivoiser les bêtes au cœur comestible, et croit entendre en lui *l'oiseau dont le chant vous fait rougir*, l'accent comme un bec-de-lièvre et la voix qui chuinte entre veille et sommeil, aussi familière que la poésie quand elle revient sans prévenir, avec ses rimes et ses réminiscences: la prime et la tierce, le lilas double au bord du pré, la lune dans un livre bilingue. Venue chercher du lait pour les morts elle s'effarouche à la moindre confidence, et quitte aussitôt la maison qu'elle hante. Courtisane qui tourne les talons, elle cache ainsi la cicatrice à son cou.

L'écho qui vient du grec, le caillou au fond du puits ont suffi pendant des siècles à mesurer la portée de sa voix. Avant la mue qui l'empêche de déclarer son nom – de cantatrice ou de revenante ébouriffée par l'air, par le vent qui s'engouffre entre rime et récit.

Son amant qui ne sait rien de son sommeil nous parle pourtant de nuits enluminées, d'une fourrure encore vivante et d'orthographe où les mots sont attachés. Le livre de la mémoire est un cahier aux marges ornées de rouge, où la main de l'enfant calligraphe hésite entre le bois et la forêt, le frère et la sœur, le suicide et la mort. C'est à cet endroit précis que le lecteur un peu plus tard glisse une lame entre les mots.

Incise ou césure, le cœur auréolé du bois mort s'ouvre à la mémoire encombrée de branches – la forêt illustrée de l'enfance et l'ébénisterie des chambres: meubles fermés à clef, tiroirs où l'on fouille pour trouver l'inutile, comme de la monnaie sans âge ou l'anneau qui ne manquait peut-être à personne – pas plus que l'aiguille ou l'os du talon retrouvé par l'archéologue: était-ce l'astragale au nom ailé, l'invisible «cheville» d'une phrase un peu bancale ou l'os en trop qui fait trébucher l'espèce?

Wood Asleep

Castle of ferns and *sleep in a nest of flames*, the forest has closed in on a sleeping beauty with an ebony face, a dead woman with crimson make-up.

Virgin unknowingly pregnant, mother of daylight and the dawn which soon will awaken her, she sleeps dreamless and speechless at the heart of the half-open book, where the child who has just learned to read looks at her furtively, finger on lips, waiting for the kiss on the mouth.

He would like to tame the beasts with an edible heart, and thinks he can hear within him the *bird whose song makes you blush*, with hare-lipped tones and a voice half-hooting half-hissing between waking and sleeping, as familiar as poetry returning without warning with its rhymes and reminiscences: the bonus and the straight flush, double lilac on the edge of the meadow, the moon in a bilingual book. Poetry come to seek milk for the dead is startled away at the slightest confidence, and flees in a trice the house it haunts: a courtisan turning on her heels to hide the scar on her neck.

The echo coming from the Greek, the pebble at the bottom of the well have been enough for centuries to measure the reach of her voice. Before it broke preventing her from declaring her name – that of singer or spectre dishevelled by the air, by the wind rushing in between song and story.

Her lover who knows nothing of how she sleeps tells us nonetheless of illuminated nights, a living fur and a spelling where the words are joined up. The book of memory is an exercise book with margins embellished in red, where the hand of the child calligrapher wavers between wood and forest, brother and sister, suicide and death. At this very place, a little later, the reader slips a knife between the words.

Interpolation or caesura, the haloed heart of the dead wood opens up to memory tangled up in branches – the illustrated forest of childhood and the panelling of bedrooms: locked cabinets, fumbling in drawers in search of the futile, such as age-old coins or the ring that perhaps no one knew was lost – any more than the needle or the heel bone discovered by the archaeologist: was it the astragalus with its winged name, the invisible "padding" in a slightly lopsided sentence, or the redundant bone that trips up the species?

Bloodaxe Contemporary French Poets

Series Editors: **Timothy Mathews & Michael Worton**

FRENCH-ENGLISH BILINGUAL EDITIONS

1: **Yves Bonnefoy:** *On the Motion and Immobility of Douve / Du mouvement et de l'immobilité de Douve*
Trans. Galway Kinnell. Introduction: Timothy Mathews. £7.95

2: **René Char:** *The Dawn Breakers / Les Matinaux*
Trans. & intr. Michael Worton. £7.95

3: **Henri Michaux:** *Spaced, Displaced / Déplacements Dégagements*
Trans. David & Helen Constantine. Introduction: Peter Broome. £7.95

4: **Aimé Césaire:** *Notebook of a Return to My Native Land / Cahier d'un retour au pays natal*
Trans. & intr. Mireille Rosello (with Annie Pritchard). £8.95

5: **Philippe Jaccottet:** *Under Clouded Skies / Beauregard Pensées sous les nuages / Beauregard*
Trans. David Constantine & Mark Treharne.
Introduction: Mark Treharne. £8.95

6: **Paul Éluard:** *Unbroken Poetry II / Poésie ininterrompue II*
Trans. Gilbert Bowen. Introduction: Jill Lewis. £8.95

7: **André Frénaud:** *Rome the Sorceress / La Sorcière de Rome*
Trans. Keith Bosley. Introduction: Peter Broome. £8.95

8: **Gérard Macé:** *Wood Asleep / Bois dormant*
Trans. David Kelley with Timothy Mathews.
Introduction: Jean-Pierre Richard. £8.95

9: **Guillevic:** *Carnac*
Trans. John Montague. Introduction: Stephen Romer. £8.95

10: **Salah Stétié:** *Cold Water Shielded: Selected Poems*
Trans. & intr. Michael Bishop. £9.95

'Bloodaxe's Contemporary French Poets series could not have arrived at a more opportune time, and I cannot remember any translation initiative in the past thirty years that has been more ambitious or more coherently planned in its attempt to bring French poetry across the Channel and the Atlantic. Under the editorship of Timothy Mathews and Michael Worton, the series has a clear format and an even clearer sense of mission' – MALCOLM BOWIE, *TLS*

YVES BONNEFOY
On the Motion and Immobility of Douve:
Du mouvement et de l'immobilité de Douve
Translated by Galway Kinnell. Introduction by Timothy Mathews.

Yves Bonnefoy is a central figure in post-war French culture. Born in 1923, he has had a lifelong fascination with the problems of translation. Language, for him, is a visceral, intensely material element in our existence, and yet the abstract quality of words distorts the immediate, material quality of our contact with the world.

This concern with what separates words from an essential truth hidden in objects involves him in wide-ranging philosophical and theological investigations of the spiritual and the sacred. But for all his intellectual drive and rigour, Bonnefoy's poetry is essentially of the concrete and the tangible, and addresses itself to our most familiar and intimate experiences of objects and of each other.

In his first book of poetry, published in France in 1953, Bonnefoy reflects on the value and mechanism of language in a series of short variations on the life and death of a much loved woman, Douve. In his introduction, Timothy Mathews shows how Bonnefoy's poetics are enmeshed with his philosophical, religious and critical thought.

Galway Kinnell is one of America's leading poets. His *Selected Poems* (1982) won the National Book Award and the Pulitzer Prize. His *Selected Poems* was published by Bloodaxe in 2001.

RENÉ CHAR
The Dawn Breakers:
Les Matinaux
Edited & translated by Michael Worton

René Char (1907-88) is generally regarded as one of the most important modern French poets. Admired by Heidegger for the profundity of his poetic philosophy, he was also a hero of the French Resistance and in the 1960s a militant anti-nuclear protester.

Associated with the Surrealist movement for several years and a close friend of many painters – notably Braque, Giacometti and Picasso – he wrote poetry which miraculously, often challengingly, confronts the major 20th century moral, political and artistic concerns with a simplicity of vision and expression that owes much to the poet-philosophers of ancient Greece.

Les Matinaux (1947-49) is perhaps his greatest collection. Published after the War, it looks forward to a better and freer world, whilst also bearing the marks of a deep-seated hatred of all fascisms. It contains some of the most beautiful love poems ever written in French.

Michael Worton's translations convey the essence of Char's poetry (which says difficult things in a simple, traditional way), and his introduction suggests why Char is one of the vital voices of our age.

BLOODAXE CONTEMPORARY FRENCH POETS: 3

HENRI MICHAUX
Spaced, Displaced:
Déplacements Dégagements
Translated by David & Helen Constantine. Introduction by Peter Broome.

Henri Michaux (1899-1984) is one of the notable travellers of modern French poetry: not only to the Amazon and the Far East, but into the strange hinterland of his own inner space, the surprises and shocks of which he has never ceased to explore as a foreign country in their own right, and a language to be learned. Fired by the same explorer's appetite, he has delved into the realm of mescaline and other drugs, and his wartime poetry, part of a private "resistance" movement of extraordinary density and energy, has advertised his view of the poetic act as a form of exorcism.

His insatiable thirst for new artistic expressions of himself made him one of the most aggressive and disquieting of contemporary French painters. If he is close to anyone, it is to Klee and Pollock, but he was as much inspired by Oriental graphic arts.

Déplacements Dégagements (1985) has all the hallmarks of Michaux's most dynamic work: poetry testing itself dangerously at the frontiers, acutely analytical, linguistically versatile and full of surprising insights into previously undiscovered movements of the mind.

David Constantine has published seven books of poems with Bloodaxe, has translated poetry from French, Greek and German, and won the European Poetry Translation Prize for his *Selected Poems* of Friedrich Hölderlin. **Helen Constantine** is a freelance translator whose recent work includes editions of Théophile Gautier (Penguin Classics) and Parisian short stories (OUP). The Constantines are the new co-editors of *Modern Poetry in Translation*. **Peter Broome** recently retired as Professor of French at Queen's University, Belfast. He is co-author of *The Appreciation of Modern French Poetry* and *An Anthology of Modern French Poetry* (CUP, 1976), and author of monographs on Michaux and Frénaud.

AIMÉ CÉSAIRE
Notebook of a Return to My Native Land:
Cahier d'un retour au pays natal
Translated by Mireille Rosello with Annie Pritchard
Introduction by Mireille Rosello

André Breton called Aimé Césaire's *Cahier* 'nothing less than the greatest lyrical monument of this time'. It is a seminal text in Surrealist, French and Black literatures, only now published in full in English for the first time.

Aimé Césaire was born in 1913 in Basse-Pointe, a village on the north coast of Martinique, a former French colony in the Caribbean (now an overseas département of France). His *Notebook of a Return to My Native Land* is the foundation stone of francophone Black literature: it is here that the word *Negritude* appeared for the first time. *Negritude* has come to mean the cultural, philosophical and political movement co-founded in Paris in the 1930s by three Black students from French colonies: the poets Léon-Gontran Damas from French Guiana; Léopold Senghor, later President of Senegal; and Aimé Césaire, who became a deputy in the French National Assembly for the Revolutionary Party of Martinique and was until very recently Mayor of Fort-de-France.

As a poet, Césaire believes in the revolutionary power of language, and in the *Notebook* he combines high literary French with Martinican colloquialisms, and archaic turns of phrase with dazzling new coinages. The result is a challenging and deeply moving poem on the theme of the future of the negro race which presents and enacts the poignant search for a Martinican identity. The *Notebook* opposes the ideology of colonialism by inventing a language that refuses assimilation to a dominant cultural norm, a language that teaches resistance and liberation.

Mireille Rosello lectures in French at Northwestern University, USA. Her books, all in French, include *Littérature et identité créole aux Antilles*, and studies of André Breton and Michel Tournier.

'Aimé Césaire's *Notebook of a Return to My Native Land* is one of the most extraordinary written this century... *Notebook* is a declaration of independence...As ambitious as Joyce, Césaire sets out to "forge the uncreated conscience" of his race...Rosello's introduction discusses the poem's influence on later Caribbean writers, many of whom have sought to close the gap between the literary and the vernacular that *Notebook* so vividly explores' – MARK FORD, *Guardian*

PHILIPPE JACCOTTET

Under Clouded Skies / Beauregard
Pensées sous les nuages / Beauregard

Translated by Mark Treharne & David Constantine
Introduction by Mark Treharne
Poetry Book Society Recommended Translation

Philippe Jaccottet's poetry is meditative, immediate and sensuous. It is rooted in the Drôme region of south-east France, which gives it a rich sense of place. This book brings together his reflections on landscape in the prose pieces of *Beauregard* (1981) and in the poems of *Under Clouded Skies* (1983), two thematically linked collections which are remarkable for their lyrical restraint and quiet power.

Jaccottet's poetry is largely grounded in landscape and the visual world, pursuing an anxious and persistent questioning of natural signs, meticulously conveyed in a syntax of great inventiveness. His work is animated by a fascination with the visible world from which he translates visual objects into verbal images and ultimately into figures of language. His poems are highly attentive, pushing the eye beyond what it sees, enacting a rich hesitation between meaning conferred and meaning withheld.

Born in Switzerland in 1925, Philippe Jaccottet is one of the most prominent figures of the immediate post-war generation of French poets. He has lived in France since 1953, working as a translator and freelance writer. As well as poetry, he has published prose writings, notebooks and critical essays. He is particularly well-known as a translator from German (Musil, Rilke, Mann, Hölderlin) but has also translated Homer, Plato, Ungaretti, Montale, Góngora and Mandelstam. He has won many distinguished prizes for his work both in France and elsewhere. His *Selected Poems*, translated by Derek Mahon, was published by Penguin in 1988.

Mark Treharne taught French at the University of Warwick until 1992. He has translated much of Jaccottet's prose and written on modern French Literature. **David Constantine** has published seven books of poems and a novel with Bloodaxe, and has translated poetry from French, Greek and German. He won the European Poetry Translation Prize for his *Selected Poems* of Friedrich Hölderlin and the Corneliu M Popescu Prize for European Poetry Translation for his translation of Hans Magnus Enzensberger's *Lighter Than Air* (Bloodaxe, 2002). The translators worked in close collaboration with Philippe Jaccottet on this edition.

PAUL ÉLUARD

Unbroken Poetry II

Poésie ininterrompue II

Translated by Gilbert Bowen
Introduction by Jill Lewis

Paul Éluard's poetry is concerned with sexual desire and the desire for social change. A central participant in Dada and in the Surrealist movement, Éluard joined the French Communist Party and worked actively in the Resistance in Nazi-occupied Paris. Caught between the horrors of Stalinism and post-war, right-wing anticommunism, his writing sustains an insistent vision of poetry as a multi-faceted weapon against injustice and oppression. For Éluard, poetry is a way of infiltrating the reader with greater emotional awareness of the social problems of the modern world.

Unbroken Poetry II, published posthumously in 1953, pays tribute to Dominique Éluard, with whom Paul spent the last years of his life. It traces the internal dialogues of a passionate relationship as well as of his continuing re-evaluation of the poetic project itself. It centres on political commitment and places it at the heart of the lovers' desire.

Gilbert Bowen's other translations include *Paul Éluard: Selected Poems* (John Calder, 1987). He died in 1996. **Jill Lewis** is Associate Professor of Literature and Feminist Studies at Hampshire College, Amherst, Massachusetts. She is co-author of *Common Differences: conflicts in black and white feminist perspectives*, and wrote a book on Paul Éluard entitled *Of Politics and Desire*.

ANDRÉ FRÉNAUD

Rome the Sorceress

La Sorcière de Rome

Translated by Keith Bosley. Introduction by Peter Broome.
Poetry Book Society Recommended Translation

First known for his war-time poems written from a German labour camp – notably his sombre reworkings of the myth of the Magi – André Frénaud (1907-1993) is one of the most searching of French poets. His work is structured by a sense of quest, which gives it its labyrinthine patterns, underground tensions and fractured, inventive forms. His poetry has an epic and tragic dimension: spurred by an urge for transcendence, it refuses false paradises, arrivals and notions of reconciliation.

Rome the Sorceress (1973) is Frénaud's richest and most disturbing confrontation with the hidden life of myths and the sacred, probing the themes of time, inheritance, revolt, illusions of divinity, father-figures, mother-figures, and the insatiable monuments of language which pretend to grapple with this weight of experience.

'Frénaud is a strong and original French poet who deserves to be much better known in this country. This book uses the city of Rome as a focus for an impassioned meditation on culture and barbarism, faiths and revolts, cruelties and aspirations. Pagan and Christian forces come alike under the burning-glass in a work of immediate impact, even if at times dark and enigmatic' – EDWIN MORGAN, *Poetry Book Society Bulletin*.

BLOODAXE CONTEMPORARY FRENCH POETS: 9

GUILLEVIC
Carnac
Translated by John Montague
Introduction by Stephen Romer

One of France's most important contemporary poets, Guillevic (1907-1997) was born in Carnac in Brittany, and although he never learned the Breton language, his personality is deeply marked by his feeling of oneness with his homeland. His poetry has a remarkable unity, driven by his desire to use words to bridge a tragic gulf between man and a harsh and often apparently hostile natural environment. For Guillevic, the purpose of poetry is to arouse the sense of Being. In this poetry of description – where entire landscapes are built up from short, intense texts – language is reduced to its essentials, as words are placed on the page 'like a dam against time'. When reading these poems, it is as if time is being stopped for man to find himself again.

Carnac (1961) marks the beginning of Guillevic's mature life as a poet. A single poem in several parts, it evokes the rocky, sea-bound, unfinished landscape of Brittany with its sacred objects and its great silent sense of waiting. The texts are brief but have a grave, meditative serenity, as the poet seeks to effect balance and to help us 'to make friends with nature' and to live in a universe which is chaotic and often frightening.

John Montague is one of Ireland's leading poets. He has published three books of poetry with Bloodaxe, and his *Collected Poems* with Gallery Press. He translated Francis Ponge's *Selected Poems* with C.K. Williams and Margaret Guiton (Wake Forest University Press, USA & Faber, UK). **Stephen Romer** is Maître de Conferences at the University of Tours, and published three collections, *Idols*, *Plato's Ladder* and *Tribute*, with OUP. He translated Jacques Dupin's *Selected Poems* with Paul Auster and David Shapiro (Wake Forest University Press, USA & Bloodaxe Books, UK).

BLOODAXE CONTEMPORARY FRENCH POETS: 10
UNESCO COLLECTION OF REPRESENTATION WORKS

SALAH STÉTIÉ
Cold Water Shielded: Selected Poems
Edited & translated by Michael Bishop

Salah Stétié is a French Lebanese poet and essayist of international renown. In his exquisite, soberly beautiful poems, Western culture merges with Oriental and Arabic traditions. His writing has a swirling metaphysical dimension while never ceasing to root itself in earthy, sensuous experience. His poems evoke a deep, half-questioning, half-serene meditation of all that is 'hanging on the other side of being' – 'the great soft lion's track in the invisible' – while still capturing the swarming particularities of our daily presence in the world.

Salah Stétié was born in Beirut in 1929. After studies in Lebanon and France, he turned his attention towards the problems of contemporary poetry, establishing exchanges and friendships with writers such as Jouve, Mandiargues, Ungaretti, Bonnefoy, Du Bouchet and David Gascoyne. After launching the cultural weekly *L'Orient littéraire* in Beirut, he developed two parallel careers, as a writer and as a distinguished diplomat, in Paris, Morocco, The Hague and elsewhere. He has published 40 books, and was awarded Le Grand Prix de la Francophonie in 1995.

Michael Bishop is McCulloch Professor of French at Dalhousie University, Halifax, Canada. His many studies, anthologies and editions of modern and contemporary French poetry include books on Deguy and Char.

Other French Editions from Bloodaxe

FRENCH-ENGLISH BILINGUAL EDITIONS

JACQUES DUPIN
Selected Poems
Translated by Paul Auster, Stephen Romer & David Shapiro

Jacques Dupin was born in 1927 in Privas in the Ardèche. Images of the harsh mineral nakedness of his native countryside run through the whole of his work and figure a fundamental existential nakedness. Dupin is an ascetic who likes the bare and the simple. His poetry is sad, wise and relentlessly honest. He speaks in our ear, as if at once close and far off, to tell us what we knew: 'Neither passion nor possession'.

He is a poet and art critic, and a formidable authority on the work of Miró and Giacometti. This edition of his prose poems and lyrics has been selected by Paul Auster from seven collections published between 1958 and 1982, culminating in his *Songs of Rescue*. It has an introduction by Mary Ann Caws, Professor of French at City University of New York.

PIERRE REVERDY
Selected Poems
Translated by John Ashbery, Mary Ann Caws & Patricia Terry
Edited by Timothy Bent & Germaine Brée

Pierre Reverdy (1889-1960) is one of the greatest and most influential figures in modern French poetry. He founded the journal *Nord-Sud* with Max Jacob and Guillaume Apollinaire, which drew together the first Surrealists. Associated with painters such as Picasso, Gris and Braque, he has been called a Cubist poet, for conventional structure is eliminated in his *poésie brut* ('raw poetry'), much as the painters cut away surface appearance to bring through the underlying forms. But Reverdy went beyond Cubist desolation to express a profound spiritual doubt and his sense of a mystery in the universe forever beyond his understanding.

André Breton hailed him in the first Surrealist Manifesto as 'the greatest poet of the time'. Louis Aragon said that for Breton, Soupault, Éluard and himself, Reverdy was 'our immediate elder, the exemplary poet'.

JEAN TARDIEU
The River Underground:
Selected Poems & Prose
Translated by David Kelley

The poetry of **Jean Tardieu** (1903-95) has an almost child-like simplicity, and in France his work is studied both in universities and in primary schools. Yet while he was a household name in France and has been translated into most European languages, his poetry remains little known in the English-speaking world, despite its immediacy and sense of fun.

In his early years the difficulties of writing lyric poetry in a schizophrenic age led Tardieu to a multiplication of poetic voices, and so to working for the stage, and he was writing what was subsequently dubbed 'Theatre of the Absurd' before Beckett's and Ionesco's plays had ever been performed.

This selection includes the sequence *Space and the Flute* (1958), which Tardieu wrote for drawings by his friend Pablo Picasso. Their poems and drawings are reproduced together in this edition, which spans 80 years of Tardieu's writing.

ALISTAIR ELLIOT
French Love Poems
Poetry Book Society Recommended Translation

French Love Poems is about the kinds of love that puzzle, delight and afflict us throughout our lives, from going on walks with an attractive cousin before Sunday dinner (Nerval) to indulging a granddaughter (Hugo). On the way there's the first yes from lips we love (Verlaine), a sky full of stars reflected fatally in Cleopatra's eyes (Heredia), lying awake waiting for your lover (Valéry), and the defeated toys of dead children (Gautier).

The selection covers five centuries, from Ronsard to Valéry. Other poets represented include Baudelaire, Mallarmé, Rimbaud, La Fontaine, Laforgue and Leconte de Lisle. The 35 poems, chosen by Alistair Elliot, are printed opposite his own highly skilful verse translations. There are also helpful notes on French verse technique and on points of obscurity.

THE NEW FRENCH POETRY

Edited & translated by

David Kelley & Jean Khalfa

This anthology captures the excitement of one of the most challenging developments in contemporary French writing, the new metaphysical poetry which has become an influential strand in recent French literature. It is a rigorously ontological poetry concerned with the very being of things, and with the nature of poetic language itself.

This is not the only kind of poetry being written in France today, but it is an extremely significant development, not only in French poetry, but also in French writing as a whole. Indeed, some of the writers included in this book, notably Édmond Jabès and Gérard Macé, have been influential in the subversion of conventional *genres*, by the play between poetry, narrative and essay, which has been an important aspect of recent French literature.

This anthology brings together writers of difference generations, from Gisèle Prassinos and Joyce Mansour, through Jacques Dupin and Bernard Noël, to Franck-André Jamme and André Velter. It represents those who are major figures in France and already have some reputation in Britain and America, alongside writers who are still relatively unknown to English readers. Much of the poetry shows an affinity with the work of Henri Michaux. The book also reflects the range of poetry published by the innovative French imprint Éditions Fata Morgana, as well as the lists of leading French publishers such as Gallimard, Éditions du Seuil and Mercure de France.

David Kelley was Senior Lecturer in French and Director of Studies in Modern Languages at Trinity College, Cambridge. He died in 1999. His translations include Jean Tardieu's *The River Underground: Selected Poems & Prose* (Bloodaxe Books, 1991) and Gérard Macé's *Wood Asleep* (with Timothy Mathews) in the Bloodaxe Contemporary French Poets series. **Jean Khalfa** is a distinguished French scholar and a former diplomat. He is currently a Fellow of Trinity College, Cambridge.

PAUL VALÉRY
La Jeune Parque
Translated by Alistair Elliot

'A poem should not mean, but be,' said Archibald MacLeish. *La Jeune Parque* ('the goddess of Fate as a young woman') certainly exists: she's beautiful and makes great gestures. And as for what she means, there's a substantial amount of argument about that, so *La Jeune Parque* is a poem by either definition. It's a classic, by general agreement, written to the full 17th-century recipe for alexandrine couplets, and it's modern, with every word pulling its weight in more than one direction.

Alistair Elliot's parallel translation with notes is aimed at making this rewarding but difficult long poem accessible enough for bafflement to turn into admiration. He attempts to clarify its small puzzles and also trace the overall narrative line of Paul Valéry's poem: it does have a story (what should a young woman do?) and does struggle towards a resolution. He also provides an introduction which deals with the interesting circumstances of the poem's four-year composition (1913-17), which resulted in Valery's instantly becoming a famous poet at the age of forty-five, after having written no poetry for twenty years.

This is Alistair Elliot's fifth book of verse translation – the others being Verlaine's *Femmes/Hombres* (Anvil), Heine's *The Lazarus Poems* (MidNAG/Carcanet), and *French Love Poems* and *Italian Landscape Poems* (both Bloodaxe). He has also edited a parallel-text version of Virgil's *Georgics* with Dryden's translation (MidNAG), and translated Euripides' *Medea*, the basis of Diana Rigg's prize-winning performances at the Almeida Theatre (1992) and elsewhere. His own Collected Poems, *My Country* (1989), and his latest collections *Turning the Stones* (1993) and *Facing Things* (1997), are published by Carcanet.